An Encyclopedia by Women for Women
(and Those Who Love Them)

Unveiling the Secrets

Shana Hartman & Cindy Urbanski, Editors

Synergy Publishing Group
Belmont, North Carolina

Unveiling the Secrets: An Encyclopedia by Women for Women (and Those Who Love Them)

Edited by Shana V. Hartman and Cindy Urbanski

Published by Synergy Publishing Group, Belmont, NC

Cover by Arielle Torkelson

Softcover, September 2023, ISBN 978-1-960892-05-8
E-book, September 2023, 978-1-960892-06-5

Dedication

To our sisters, our mothers, our daughters,
and all those who seek Truth.

Contents

Foreword

WE RECOGNIZE THAT WE, THE AUTHORS and editors of this collection of words, do not and cannot fully represent *all* experiences and understandings of those who identify as "women." We also clearly recognize that the majority of the women authors in this collection fall into a white, middle class, heteronormative sociocultural category, and, thus, present a potentially limited perspective. We claim this reality, but are eager to engage other perspectives as well; therefore, we invite you to please follow us on Instagram @shanahartman_ and tag us in your own story with #unveilingthesecrets. We'll see you there!

Astounded

Cindy Urbanski

SECRETS.

In one of our Synergy Publishing Group team meetings in January 2023, we started kicking around the idea for our next collaborative book project. As we reminisced on the joy we experienced writing with a group of women authors in a previous collaborative book, *Capturing the In-Between* (2022), we got curious as to what else we women had to share with the world. What are the things that are "not said" and "not talked about" to women that would have been *so* helpful to know as we became women? What could have been shared that would have saved us women from moments of trauma, heartache, pain, and good old fashioned embarrassment?

All a girl has to do is read Anita Diamant's *Red Tent* to know that women know things and have wisdom to drop. They know the secrets. But, Red Tent gatherings ceased long ago. We have become more isolated, busier, and less transparent without those moments of respite.

So, what if we invited women into our own version of the Red Tent in the form of a multi-genre, multi-generational collaborative book? What might happen?

Oh yes, we had ideas and visions, sure. Yet, what we received from these amazing women was beyond what we had imagined.

When women come together and have the courage to be vulnerable, magic happens.

As I read and responded to these amazing writings, I started to wonder where this courage comes from. It occurred to me that maybe it was the community, but more so, maybe it was the invitation to teach—to reach out to other women of all ages and say, "I've got you. Let my experience help you get through your own." And in writing that story, maybe there was some healing for each of the writers themselves.

So, we invite you into our world of secrets. We organized each unveiled secret alphabetically to mimic an encyclopedia by women for women (and those who love them). As such, you can read this book in the order provided or bounce around, dwelling and returning to "letters" as you see fit.

Brain Damage

Melisa Graham

*Trigger Warning: Intrusive thoughts and suicidal
ideation are present in this story.*

GET IT TOGETHER, YOU DUMB BITCH, said the voice in my head that
sounded remarkably like me. *You're such a waste of space. Why don't
you just die?*

We were having an especially bad day, my brain and I. Nothing
bad had happened, per se. My brain had just gone off the rails on
a random Tuesday and dragged the rest of me along with it.

I learned recently, at age 48, that the life-long depression
and anxiety I've experienced was likely due to undiagnosed,
unmanaged attention-deficit/hyperactivity disorder (ADHD) and
autism spectrum disorder (ASD), or as those in the neurodivergent
community online have dubbed it, AuDHD. I'd been treating
the depression with a combination of talk therapy, cognitive
behavioral therapy, and dialectical behavior therapy on and
off since age 12. In my late 20s, my primary doctor suggested
the antidepressant Wellbutrin since my symptoms often left me
sluggish and unmotivated. Then, some time in my early 40s, she
prescribed Xanax when I described what happened in my body
when my ex or my boss called me.

These therapies and medications helped, but nothing seemed to cure. I figured my brain was just defective and learned how to spot when it was going off the rails. Then I'd try a series of interventions to get it back on track, a process that could take days or even weeks. Hell, sometimes years, especially when the derailment left my body mangled: like the time I dislocated my jaw because the tissues were worn down from my constant clenching and grinding; or when the chronic stress impacted my histamine levels, and I discovered I was allergic to most skin care and beauty products; or when I'm too tired to think straight but too wired on anxiety to sleep.

When I'd woken up that random Tuesday morning in my 48th year—a full 8 months after my ADHD diagnosis and starting on Vyvanse—my husband said something that sent me into a spiral. He didn't mean to make me feel bad, and I knew it. But sometimes one part of my brain can know something while another part firmly insists otherwise. In this particular instance, I think the ASD took over with a rigid, literal interpretation.

My husband, Todd, and I were talking about a stray kitty, with an injured tail, who was tugging on my emotions. I wanted to catch her and take her to the vet and then take her in. He was on board with taking her to the vet to make sure she was okay and to see if she was chipped. But he didn't want to spend a lot of money and completely shut down any discussion of adopting her. He asked, "Do you want to live in the woods with her?" He said it in a joking tone. He wouldn't really kick me out for adopting a cat. He just meant that the cat wasn't coming inside. Period. His intentions aside, the idea that he might kick me out—that he literally meant that my choice was between living inside with him or outside with the cat—set off every ounce of insecurity and low self-esteem in my body.

The fact is that he could kick me out if he wanted to. It's his house, purchased while we were dating but long before he stopped introducing me as a friend. When he eventually did invite me and my children to move in, the deal was that I would save the money I'd been spending on rent to fund future vacations.

Just a few weeks after I moved in, I was called into my supervisor's office at work where she and the CFO were waiting for me. The CFO told me I could voluntarily resign, say I was laid off, or say I was fired; either way, I had to clean out my desk and be gone immediately. The reason they gave me: I was a long-standing problem child whose most recent violation was forgetting to set my out-of-office message when I'd taken vacation time to move and then got the flu and had to take sick time. I was out for 3 weeks and missed an important assignment, which made a higher-ranked coworker look bad.

My initial thoughts overlapped: *Todd is going to hate you and kick you out. You kept your deal with him for a single paycheck, you fucking loser. What kind of horrible person gets asked to resign? What kind of idiot forgets to set her out-of-office? You fucked up, and now your already overworked colleagues will have to pick up your slack. They're going to hate you, too. Everyone will know what a loser you are, and you'll never work in this town again.*

Like a great big idiot, I chose to say I was resigning and negotiated staying another 2 weeks to prepare a transition notebook and train my colleagues on how to do my job. My supervisor kept telling me to spend the time looking for another job, but I spent all of my time on other people. Spending company time looking for another job would break some rule that I believed was real and serious.

Todd didn't kick me out after that job loss. He was clearly disappointed but said all the right things. I spent the next 6 months applying for jobs and sitting through painful interviews. I knew I bombed every single one. How do you sell yourself to strangers when your internal monologue is a constant litany of everything you've ever done wrong?

Every job I'd ever successfully landed was the result of a personal connection. The interviews were always with a family member, a close family friend, or had a familiar industry colleague present. They knew me. They knew my work ethic. They'd tell the person responsible for hiring that I was shy or quiet but super smart. And that worked out great for over a decade, from my teens to age 30. But then things just got harder and harder.

I worked full-time while caring for two small children and my fully adult first husband. He had discovered that practicing law was not for him and decided to be an entrepreneur instead. That didn't work out well for our bank account. I now know that undiagnosed, unmanaged bipolar disorder was informing a lot of his decisions. I knew that I constantly had to navigate his moods and that he too suffered from bouts of depression and anxiety, but I had no idea how our melange of mental disorders were working against us.

I also now know that I'd been wearing a mask of normalcy for a very long time, and it was slipping. I once described myself to a coworker as a chameleon: I blended in with the wallpaper in most situations, invisible and content observing. Once I got comfortable with a group, I was more outgoing, but I seemed to have a slightly different personality depending on the group. She knew exactly what I meant and felt she did something similar, but she told me that in my case, she didn't think it was working. Some of the descriptors floating around the office about me included *quirky, quiet, mean, nice, smart, sad,* and *mad.*

This chameleon life, also called "masking," is a common theme among neurodivergent folk. ("Neurodivergent" is a nonmedical, umbrella term for people whose brains develop or work differently from the "neurotypical" majority.) We often don't realize we're masking. It's ingrained from our earliest days in reprimands from our caregivers and teachers: Stop fidgeting. Pay attention. Be quiet. Stay in line. Look at me when I talk to you. Stop walking like that. Did you lose your keys again? Why are you always late? Follow the rules because I say so; stop questioning them.

I've only mastered three of these demands so far. I can fake the others for a moderate amount of time, but then I have to go home, put on cozy pants, lie down somewhere dark and quiet, and dissociate.

When I first mentioned to friends that I thought I might be ADHD and/or autistic, they said some version of, "ADHD absolutely, but not autistic; you're so caring and empathetic." I then discovered that nearly every one of my close friends has ADHD. Some had been diagnosed for a while. Others sought diagnosis as we talked more about the symptoms and efficacy of medication. I suspect some of them are autistic as well but have a skewed view of what autism looks like based on old research and stereotypes. In truth, it's a spectrum that includes a wide number of traits. When you picture this spectrum, think of a 3D, rainbow-hued ball. I'm somewhere in there.

My first-born daughter is the one who initially suggested I might be autistic. She thinks she is as well and looked into formal diagnosis. The availability of qualified health care providers makes formal diagnosis difficult. It's also probably unnecessary unless you're seeking specialized therapy or formal accommodations. Within the autistic community that I follow on social media, self-diagnosis is widely accepted and even encouraged given the difficulty of formal diagnosis. So my daughter proceeded to give herself accommodations and adapt her environment to her needs. She's now feeling better than she ever has and even cut back on her antidepressant dosage.

When I first looked at the assessments available online, I agonized over the way many of the questions were phrased, so I gave up and didn't complete them. I learned from social media that overanalyzing the questions and answers was a sign all by itself. Then I learned that if my answer was qualified by a "because" statement, my real answer was the opposite. A few examples:

- Do you frequently misplace things? No, because I now keep them in a specific place and always return them to that place … oh, then yes.

- Are you frequently late for appointments? No, because I put them on my mobile phone calendar and always set three reminders (one day before, two hours before, and time to leave) and use Google maps to tell me the optimal time to leave based on traffic patterns that time of day … oh, then yes.
- Do you have a hard time understanding idiomatic phrases like "you're the apple of my eye"? No, because I picture an apple tree in my head, and it's red and in high contrast to the background of green leaves, so my eye is drawn to it. So the phrase means that the person is like an apple and stands out from other people as something appealing that I want to pluck and bite … oh, wow, I'm overanalyzing this, so yes. And also, I really want to bite people when I like them a lot.

That last one is about literal thinking. It has come up in my marriage many times, not just on random Tuesdays. I only learned to pick up on my husband's sarcasm after *years* of study. It's so subtle, y'all. Sometimes when he tells a joke, he pauses, counting to himself, as he waits for me to pierce through the literal meaning. He also likes to use colorful phrases that he learned in the navy. My least favorite is "dicking the dog." It means "making a horrible mistake," and I know that, but my brain immediately goes to emergency room horror stories. I think it's the most nauseating idiom in the English language.

The ADHD and autistic communities online have been my saviors. They've helped me recognize that I'm not insane or defective. I'm just a dodecahedron that society has been trying to jam into a round hole for nearly 50 years. And now my edges are scratched up and worn down. It's gonna take time to polish those out, especially as I unmask and learn to manage the internal conflicts that arise when my ADHD and ASD traits clash, like when my ASD thrives on routine and order, but my ADHD constantly seeks all things new and different.

Even though both ADHD and ASD are classified as brain disorders, my brain isn't damaged. It's simply wired differently. Relative to my "normal" peers, I'm better able to perceive the subtle connections that weave the world together. I can hyperfocus on interesting problems and their solutions. If there's a weird smell or an annoying buzz, I won't rest until I find where it's coming from and eliminate it. I can organize the hell out of your closet; just don't ask me to be consistently responsible for keeping it clean. And if you find my facial expression inscrutable and perhaps off-putting, don't assume I'm sad or mad or tell me to smile. Maybe just ask me what I'm thinking and be prepared for either a few dozen random thoughts or a detailed info dump.

I wish I knew all this earlier in life. I'm sharing my experiences and reflections now in hopes that it helps other women who need to hear this. You are not damaged. You are simply wired differently. And we love that about us!

P.S. This whole rambling trail of thought began with a stray cat. I think that was probably the ADHD talking.

Call Me Mama

Shana Hartman

No one prepares you for the first time you hear the word "Mama" and realize it is directed at you.

That tiny voice working hard to coordinate with the pressing together of precious little lips and pressing down a wiggly little tongue to make the buzzing "Mmmmmaaaammmaaaaa" sound.

And, your heart all but stops.

This is who you are now. Period.

You are a Mama, Mom, Mother, Ma.

If you are lucky, you have some concept of this role of Mama due to a motherly figure—whether biological or otherwise—who has been in your life at some point. Yet, when it's your turn, when those words are turned towards you, the impact is different.

And, your world *is* different, at least in many ways compared to your pre-Mama. What we often don't realize, no matter how well it is or is not modeled for us, is that when you take on the role of Mama, you also take on the role of…

- Caregiver
- Feeder
- Soother
- Solver
- Cleaner
- Washer

- Singer
- Reader
- Bedtime tucker
- No more sleeper
- Tear dryer
- Relationship figure-outer

And the list goes on. Don't get me wrong: this Mama gig is amazing and filled with so much joy. Because while you are all of the above things that can be challenging, you are also the source of…

- Joy
- Love
- Friendship
- Healing

Still, I do wish we talked more about the identity loss that often happens. I'll start by sharing my story, which is really scary because it is not all sunshine and rainbows.

My son was barely 2 years old when *it* hit. I call *it* my very late postpartum depression moment (which we now know can last from birth up to 7 years postpartum!). My family was in the full summertime swing, and I was learning how to navigate keeping a toddler, along with the rest of my family, happy, healthy, and thriving.

I suddenly could not recognize any part of myself outside of all of the doing and being for others, and this realization caused me to go dark. Like when the old TVs from the 80s just suddenly went kaput and the picture just disappeared, leaving only a black screen behind. I felt like I was the black screen and the world was closing in on me. No warning, just darkness.

I distinctly recall one moment when I was home by myself and had just gotten my toddler to bed (finally!). I was trying to wind down with some Netflix when the darkness, the blackness, just came flooding into my brain. I closed my eyes in an attempt to get reconnected and calm myself, but that only made the darkness grow stronger. I struggled to catch my breath. I could not see my way out of all of the intense sensations bombarding me.

I needed help.

I needed some Mama-ing for me like I had been doing for others for so long.

I needed to find who I was now because of and in spite of my Mama status. I will never forget this moment where "Mama" was the very last thing I wanted to be.

No, this did not mean I didn't love my kids.

No, this did not mean I was not grateful.

No, this did not mean I was not a good mother.

It simply meant I was stuck and needed something to shift because the darkness was present and powerful. Luckily, I was able to receive the support I needed to get out of the darkness and, ultimately, redefine me, my Mama status, and so much more. My steps were not unique or magical, and yet they guided me, emotion by emotion through my healing journey. But first, coffee, yes, and also *therapy*. I cannot tell you the power of having someone outside of you and your loved ones reflect back and help you constructively and intentionally work through the darkness. Therapy is now an essential part of my life forever. My family also supported me in offering to give me more breaks and listening when I finally learned to say, "I need help." Eventually, I also carved out a new career path for myself, one that aligned with how I wanted to show up and share my energy with the world.

Because I honored what was showing up for me—the dark, the depression, the lostness—I was able to be an even better version of myself, which will always make me a better Mama.

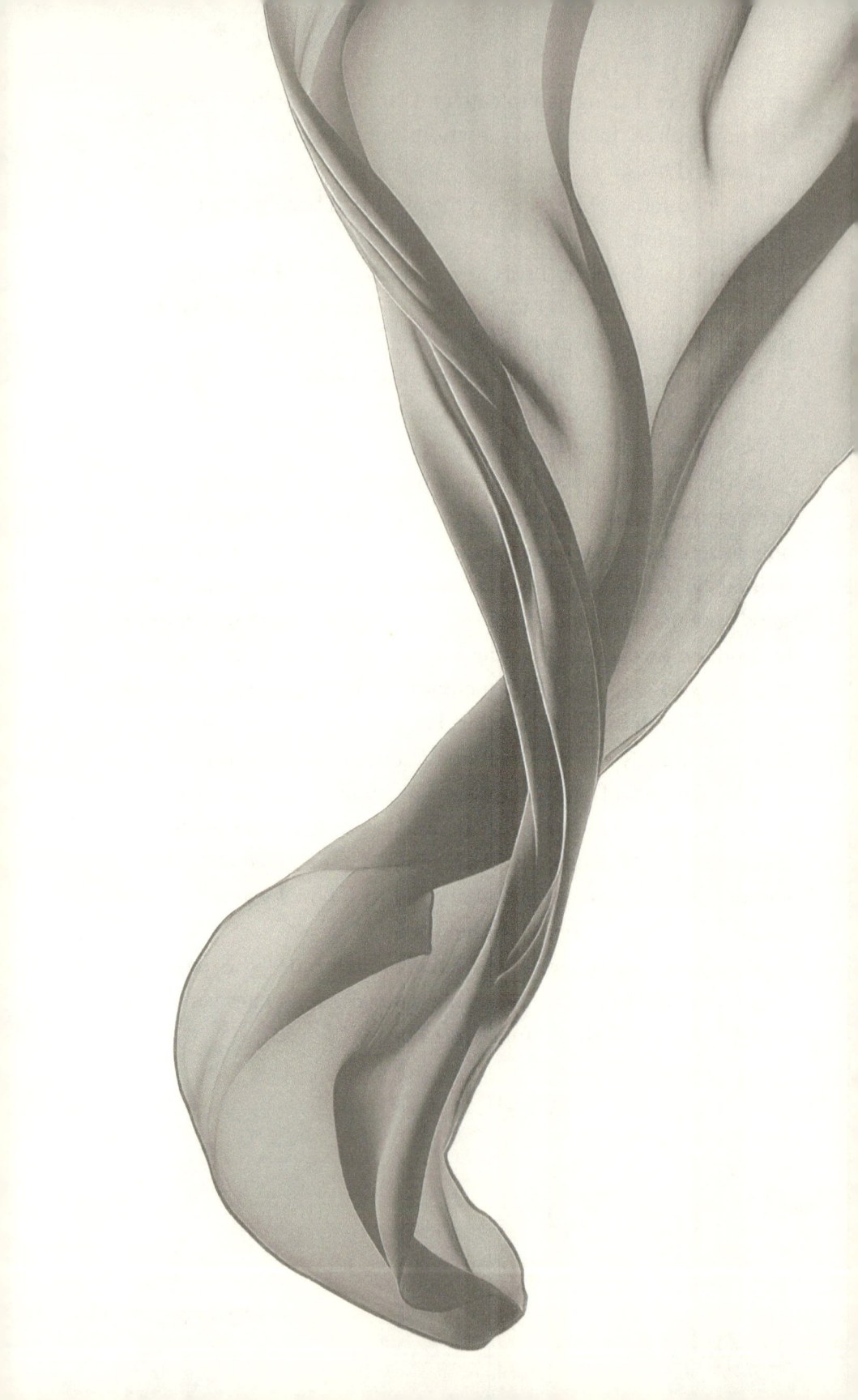

Death Becomes Her

Melisa Graham

ONE OF MY EARLIEST MEMORIES IS my death. My mom said we were going to the doctor. That was cool because Dr. Counts always gave me lollipops! We got to the doctor's office, but it was nighttime, and there were no cars in the parking lot. *Weird.* Then the memory jumps to a bright light in my face and a bushy-bearded doctor staring down at me. He wasn't Dr. Counts, and he didn't have a lollipop. *Weirder and not cool.*

For the longest time, I didn't understand the memory. I just knew it was disconcerting. Then one day I jokingly asked my mom if I'd been abducted by aliens when I was little. She gave me that look that I'm pretty sure all moms give their children when they ask ridiculous questions and said, "Why do you ask?" *That wasn't a no.* I recounted the memory for her.

"Oh, no," she said. "That wasn't aliens."

Then she filled in the details of my spotty memory. I was around 13 months old and had been very sick. Mom called her mother, my Mamaw, over to help. Mamaw lost her second child to a rare intestinal disease, so she took care of my siblings and I when we were sick, determined never to lose another baby. It seems like I was sick a lot as a kid and probably got more than my fair share of her attention. "Wellness" wasn't really a thing for my generation of semi-feral latchkey kids eating Pop-Tarts for breakfast and

Stouffer's chicken pot pies for dinner—at least until we became paranoid helicopter parents.

According to Mom, they put me in a cool bath to bring my fever down. When she told me that, I recalled another memory of a high fever and a cool bath in a pink-tiled bathroom. The shock of the cool water took my breath away. It was pure torture, but Mamaw said I had to stay put because I was very sick. *How many times was I baptized as a kid?*

The bath didn't do much for my fever, and I was having trouble keeping fluids down. Mamaw pinched the back of my hand, and my skin stayed puckered—"poor turgor," it's called. It meant I was dehydrated, so off to the hospital we went. Mamaw took the wheel, and Mom held me in her lap in the back seat. This was before children had to be in car seats, although knowing my mother, she would have held me anyway to soothe us both.

It was late at night, so the streets were fairly deserted. Mamaw may have taken some liberties with the stoplights. And speed limits. And a variety of other traffic laws.

We passed my pediatrician's office on the way to the hospital. I stayed conscious just long enough to see the dark parking lot and then, apparently, dozed off. In truth, my heart stopped.

Fortunately, the hospital was just around the corner, and they rushed me into the ER. This was back when you could go to the ER and not be triaged to death. Once I was awake, the nurses had to strap me down, so I wouldn't pull out my IV. Then they gave me a doll that had a Band-Aid on her arm right where an IV would go.

I wasn't out long enough to get brain damage. Or at least, that's what the doctor would've told my mother had she thought to ask. My current mental health tells a different story; my brain definitely seems to have a few screws loose.

I'm kind of salty about the fact that I didn't see any tunnel of light or talk to any angels who said I had to go back because I had a great purpose to fulfill. That would've been a nice affirmation. What the hell am I doing here? Whose idea was this?

I'm not absolutely sure what I believe happens to our souls—energy, consciousness, whatever you want to call it—after death. I waffle between my Christian upbringing, the mysticism I learned of in my adult years, and cold logic. I only know that certain experiences have left me with a certainty that *something* happens.

Here's the raw fact about death: it is an intrinsic part of life. Death comes for us all in the end, leaving our rotting meat suits to feed the mycelia. I find that aspect of death comforting: the dust-to-dust aspect of it all, that energy can neither be created nor destroyed, only converted to something else.

Here's one such experience that leads me to believe that this fact is true: On a whim and because my friend Amy said, "C'mon, it's fun," I did a past-life regression/guided meditation. The meditation took me backward through my birth in this life, then through a place of pure-white nothingness to a door. When I stepped through the door, I was riding in a horse-drawn cart, the kind a farmer might use to take goods into town. I looked down and saw two long, golden-brown braids and a flax apron over a faded red dress. I thought, *Why am I wearing my best dress?*

I looked out over the landscape and saw rolling hills dotted with sheep and cows. It was lovely and serene. So why was my stomach churning and my chest tight? I looked to my left and saw an older man. "Older" in this context was relative—probably 40, whereas I was only 14 or 15. He was driving the cart, staring ahead at the road, and saying nothing. He posed no obvious threat, but I was afraid of him.

Details of that life trickled into my memory (imagination?) slowly. My parents had sold me to this man, a widower, to become his new wife. I'd never met him until that day, our wedding day. And now he was carting me off to care for his home and his children and—*oh hell no!*—his needs.

The meditation then directed a jump in time to a point several months or years later. I was in a small cabin carrying a baby on my hip while stirring a pot of something on a wood-burning stove.

Another girl, not much younger than me, was performing some other household task at a nearby table. Some younger boys were chasing each other through the house and laughing.

I hated them all. Even the baby. Her diaper stank, her hands were always sticky, and for some reason, she'd scream her lungs out unless I held her nonstop.

They weren't mine. They were his, of course. Why did he need a wife when he had a perfectly good daughter to care for her younger siblings? He even went to her bed some nights. I didn't hate her for that; it was a relief to be spared. I just hated her existence. I wondered briefly if she and I would get along better if we killed him.

The meditation then directed another time jump to the moments before my death in that life. I was barely conscious and lying on my side in a shallow hole. The dirt felt cool against my skin and smelled rich and clean—a stark contrast to the stench and heat from before. I didn't catch what had happened "before." I could only feel the sensations of its aftermath.

I felt a periodic tickle against my legs as dirt was shoveled on top of me and heard the soothing, rhythmic shoosh of the shovel. *Shoosh, tickle, shoosh, tickle, shoosh, tickle.*

It's finally over, I thought as I let the sensations of reprieve wash over me.

It felt so real. Whether that was truly a memory of a past life or my imagination working extra hard, it's part of me now. I can't shake the images, the smells, the fear and hatred, or conversely, the sensation of cool earth pressed against my cheek, the flood of relief at the end. I had no fear or worry in that final moment—just bone deep relief.

Here's another one.

My paternal grandmother, Ora, had Parkinson's. As I recall, it began with a tremor in her hand and perhaps some speech difficulties—she was a woman of few words at least. My memories of her are blips and snatches of her snow-white hair, the rose-scented lotion in her bathroom, her rolling out biscuits at her metal and Formica kitchen table as sun streamed through the window, her mismatched house dresses and coats, her silent laugh apparent only when she covered her mouth and her shoulders shook, which she did a lot around my dad. I suspect his sense of humor was honed precisely for that purpose.

She eventually became bedridden and lingered in that state for years, a prisoner to her own body. Walking, talking, chewing, swallowing, and thinking clearly had all become major obstacles for her. Caring for her was a team effort involving a host of aunts, uncles, and cousins. I was in college too far away to help, so I didn't witness the decline first hand. I just got the regular reports from my mom.

Even with a big team in play, it was too much, so she was finally moved into a skilled nursing facility. I visited her there. I think she was lucid enough to know me. I gave her a kiss on her forehead, and she reached up and tucked my hair behind my ear.

The next time I saw her, maybe 6 months later, she was in the hospital with pneumonia, the leading cause of death in Parkinson's patients. My mom had called and said to get to Asheville as quickly as I could.

Almost the whole family gathered in her hospital room, spilling out into the hallway and dominating the waiting room. She was unconscious the whole time I was there, but we talked to her anyway. We listened to her labored breathing become louder and wetter and slower with long pauses in between. "The death rattle," someone said.

The aunts recruited me to rub lotion on her arms and legs to help keep her comfortable. Her legs seemed remarkably tan even though they hadn't seen the sun in goodness knows how long. I have no idea how long we were in that room. Was it hours or days? Nurses and doctors came in periodically to check her vitals, to bring an extra chair, to refill the ice. Not much else they could do.

My grandfather returned to the room with a Bible. I didn't realize he'd ever left. He thought she might be waiting for a particular passage, one she'd read to other relatives in their passing: Psalm 23. You might know it: "The Lord is my shepherd; I shall not want. ..." He read the psalm aloud to her, and we all prayed.

Then *something* happened. The precise nature of that something is debatable. My rational mind says that sunlight broke through the overcast day, streaming through the window and casting shadows along the wall. And in that precise moment, my grandmother took her last breath. The rational version, however, is not what I experienced or believed in the moment. What I actually experienced was, as best I can describe it, a miracle.

As my grandfather began reading the psalm, every hair on my body stood on end. I kept my eyes open through the psalm and the prayer and watched that intimate moment between husband and wife with all their children gathered 'round. Suddenly, light came from the head of her bed, and extra people—shadowy, barely there people—squeezed in between the aunts, uncles, and cousins, joining the family in prayer. The living cried, but the shadow people seemed to vibrate with excitement. As the light faded, so did they. So did my grandmother. She was gone. All that was left was an empty shell where she'd been. I don't know how to describe the difference between her body animated with a soul and that same empty body that began to decay within seconds. To me, it was as obvious as the nose on my face.

Oddly, what's most clearly defined my view of Death, with a capital D, is Neil Gaiman's characterizations of her in his various works. Death is always feminine. That feels right. She receives. She ripens. She shows us the way. I've begun to imagine her as a close friend I haven't seen in a long time, someone who knows all my secret selves and loves every one of them. Maybe she knows what's coming next and can't wait to show me. Or maybe she's as clueless as I am, but by damn, she's going to hold my hand tightly through the in-between to bolster me for that next big step. Either way, she'll be with me, and she always has been.

Evoking Partnership

Cindy Urbanski

A Playlist.

I: "Wildest Dreams" by Taylor Swift

I was in my kitchen chopping vegetables for dog food (yep you read that correctly) when Taylor Swift started crooning about her "Wildest Dreams." Taylor took me right back to my freshman year of high school. I was dating a boy, 4 years older than me, much wilder, and having SO.MUCH.FUN. I was skipping some school (while still making A's) and sneaking out of my house. All of the things that were very out of character for my rule-following persona, the identity that I wore that didn't quite fit the real me.

Like Taylor, I knew from the get-go that my relationship with this boy would never go anywhere. I had a whole lot of guilt around that. If I wasn't all in, what was I doing? Was this responsible behavior? My upbringing was ringing in my ears. I know my parents find it hard to believe looking back at that time, but I was listening, and their lessons were loud and clear in my head.

But, he was "handsome as hell," and I adored the way I felt in his presence. Beautiful. Wanted. And yes, freaking *smart*. It's true that I would lie awake at night worrying about my future when I was not dreaming about the next time I'd sneak out to meet this boy in the woods. I wanted college; I wanted a career. I wanted kids, and I had *big* dreams. This wild boy was not the path to making those dreams reality. At least not for me, and I knew it. I was the "responsible" one in the relationship. I was the one to declare things a bad idea and put on the brakes. Always. And I didn't *want* that role. I had a secret wild side too. That's why I was with this person to begin with, and that part of me was being smothered with the burden of "better" decision making. My gut knew someone had to behave sensibly and responsibly.

See, *all* the guilt.

But here's a secret that I've learned over the years: These wild, mad love affairs in our lives serve to teach us about ourselves.

No one told me that my fling was part of a learning curve. They just told me it was crazy at best and plain wrong at worst. Even then, no one knew that my inner wild child was not being fed; in fact, she was starving. That right there was the real "wrong" in the relationship.

That boy helped me embrace and love *my* wildest dreams. He certainly embraced his! I just didn't think I was allowed to embrace mine because, well, somebody had to be responsible!

So, here is what I want to tell Taylor Swift and what I wish someone had told a 15-year-old me: Know that your wild dreams are real, they are yours, and this fling, or affair, or first love is showing you something about who you are and what you want. Recognize that, and then go get it!

II: "You're My Home" by Billy Joel

Meanwhile, back at my kitchen dance party while pondering all of this, Taylor's jam ended, and Billy Joel started to speak to me … "When you look into my eyes, and you see the crazy gypsy in my soul. It always comes as a surprise, when I feel my withered roots begin to grow …" YES, Billy—that's what I'm talking about!

At 19 as a sophomore at the college of my dreams, and after dating a slew of responsible and *boring* boys, I embraced my wild gypsy self and decided that I didn't need a man to complete my life. My plan was to move to the remote Outer Banks of North Carolina with the wild ponies and teach school. If I decided I wanted children, I'd adopt them. If Ocracoke wasn't wild enough, I'd move. It was decided.

But then there he was in his work boots and flannel shirt, riding a motorcycle and walking a bit on the wild side. And he could talk for hours about 17th century literature while fixing the clutch on my beloved 1985 Celica. And, as it would seem, we wanted the same things out of life. Adventure, adoption, a career, maybe even a house if we really got crazy.

He looked into my eyes, saw my inner, wild-child gypsy, matched her, and together we made my first real home. I put down some trembling roots.

There were mortgages and huge, scary disappointments and problems to solve. There were bills and the paying of taxes that didn't feel very sexy. There was the parenting of toddlers and teenagers from which no one survives unscathed. And arguments (and because you are both a little wild and a lot passionate, some of them are doozies).

When I really tune in to this song, and look back on my journey, I realize the secret Billy shares with us: With the right partner, the wild love affair and the responsibility and the gypsy in your souls can all coexist.

III: "You and Me" by Dave Matthews

Still in the kitchen, Dave chimes in, "Gonna take a boat to the end of the world. And when the kids are old enough, we're going to teach them to fly. You and me together can do anything."

While my husband and I have been known to take that boat to the end of the world and relish together, we are squarely in the teaching to fly phase of life. Our kids are now 19 and 22. We are nudging them out of the nest, cheering and watching them plummet, along with our hearts. We meet them in the soft grass we've placed under them to pick them up and do it all over again. Parenting doesn't end at 18. It's a forever gig. And it's less terrifying when one does it in partnership.

And here's another secret: Partnership isn't 50/50. Sometimes it is 70/30 or even 99/1. Brené Brown says this somewhere, but we have been living it for nearly 30 years. Partnership means taking *turns* with responsibility. Partnership is taking on the world back-to-back, for sure, but it's also putting down your weapon and seeking the shelter of your other half. And getting exhausted and fearful and turning your weapon on your partner out of frustration and rage at the things of life is never, ever the answer. Truly living, loving, and growing *together* with a somebody, leaning into that somebody, sheltering in that somebody, is a sign of courage and strength. It took my inner wild girl way too long to figure that out.

Freedom

Mackenzie Urbanski Menon

"WOMAN MUST BE WOMANLY."

Many of the women before me
Had no choice in their lives.
Women were to do women's work
Were not to vote
Were only to grow and raise children.

Those women fought for a change
And were strong enough to grant
Their daughters and granddaughters
The right to power over their lives.
They opened the doors for us.

"Woman can do anything."

I was born with a choice.
Carefully crafted luck landed me
In a time and place
Where, like spoils from a garden,
Paths flourish
Briefly

for the taking.

I was told that any path was mine to take.
I could conquer any challenge,
And it became a point of pride.
Anything boys could do,
I could do better.

"Woman can be anything, just like a man."

By 10 years old, I could run, read, row
Faster, better, smarter
Than anyone that dared to try.
I was chasing the praise
But not for myself.

More independent,
louder, more wild,
Exploding out of the feminine box.
I found things about myself that I loved,
But even more, I was feeling forced.

Out of one box and into another.

A prettier box to be sure,
Decorated with glitzing pieces of shattered glass ceilings
And the brightly colored power suits
Of moms who work full time and still bring snacks to practice,
Stilettos sinking into soccer fields.

Dirtier, cooler ones too
Slicked back hair and winged eyeliner
Mixed with masculine clothes
Shots of whiskey and

Housing frat boys
at their own pong tables.

"Woman must be like a man."

I wanted to be cool
To continue upholding the
"Bad bitch" image I had cultivated
That would surely lead me straight
To the coveted Boss Mom persona.

And
I don't know their stories,
I can't claim to see their inner monologue.
But I do see
circles under their concealer
And hear
quiet sighs that slip out when asked,
"How do you do it all?"

As a teenager, I was shoving myself into that world
That shimmering box that promised
Pride, love, fulfillment—

But it was built from fear.
Fear of being perceived as lazy and ungrateful,
And failing to fill the expectations of everyone around us.

Somehow, we shifted.
How did we get back here?
Shoving ourselves back into the boxes
Our foremothers worked so hard to free us from
In the name of honoring their work?

You asked for the secret?
True Feminism believes that

"Woman is free."

Now, at a freshly minted 22 years old,
I am finally sitting with those flourishing paths
instead of running headlong through them.

I'm trusting myself to take those I want
and leave those I don't.

I find myself engaged to the love of my life,
overjoyed and unbothered
by the voices of people who will tell me
I'm moving too fast,
that by getting married I'm throwing away my career,
that I am taking steps backwards in the feminist agenda.

I know the truth.

My freedom to choose is the legacy we have been gifted.
I can do both, one, or neither.
I can pack it all in and decide I want to spend a
    year backpacking the Appalachian Trail.
Each and every path is a gift,
and each and every path is mine to take.
That feminism,
my friends,
is freedom.

Grudges

Amanda Soesbee Kent

WALLS, DOORS, AND GRUDGES.

I'm a teacher. It's not just what I do; it's who I am. I teach the teens; I teach the lessons. That's why, when from the mouth of a babe comes a "Yeah, but" moment, I experience a sense of pride followed by a dose of "I should've thought of that!" What follows is a secret shared with me by a 15-year-old student.

One year, my 10th grade students read a short story called "The Interlopers" as part of a unit on characters and conflict. Basically, the story is about two men whose families have fought for years over a plot of land. The two men don't know why they hate each other, but they do. Then, they get trapped on the land in a winter storm and have to overcome their hatred for each other in order to figure out how to escape. After reading, we talked as a class about the follies and vices of human nature that are exposed in the story—greed, selfishness, holding grudges, hatred. The students in these particular classes were on a relatively high level academically and typically shared some insightful thoughts; they made connections between the dangers of holding grudges and losing loved ones and ruining your character ... all kinds of greatness. I fluffed my tail feathers like a peacock, thinking I'd just saved the future of humanity because these kids were all agreeing and embracing kindness and conflict resolution ... until one defiant voice from the corner of the room shattered it all: "I don't know … I'm kind of a fan of a little grudge now and then."

In the next few minutes, we heard a very valid and convincing counter-argument from a 15-year-old kid explaining how he sees holding grudges as a self-preservation mechanism, and how recognizing that you're purposefully holding a grudge can actually strengthen rather than weaken your character. He said, "You gotta watch out for yourself. You're the best person to protect you. If someone's hurt you, you'd better be careful before you let them back in!" First and foremost, I'm concerned that our future generation is already worried about protecting themselves against the dangers of humanity's attacks on one another. We don't realize how inundated they are with hate, and it makes me sad. But, I also thought about how smart this kid actually was in this moment; he was able to see past the author's intended message and relate the story to the world he lives in.

Which made me wonder …

What are the best ways to protect yourself? (Not physically. Please, by all means, take the self-defense classes and buy the alarm systems and get the dogs, whatever you need to do. But I'm talking about emotional protection here.) Some people shut down completely. Some people cut others out of their lives. Some people's defense is an angry offense. And yes, for some people like me and this student, protection means holding grudges by constructing metaphorical walls around the heart. I still tend to think like a single woman because I was one for most of my life, so this conversation isn't going to be the same for many folks. But ya know, it needs to happen.

I had an awesome chat the other day about "walls," and how it's not fair to the people who aren't responsible for them when you put them up. But what else you gon' do? If you don't put up the walls or hold the grudges, how do you protect your heart and soul from a constant barrage of emotional attacks? I think it's vitally important to recognize that protective element within ourselves, because we all have one, and be prepared to look for the same in others. And once you recognize it, question why it's there. That's the basis for beginning to understand one another.

In my humblest of opinions, it's okay for women to be protective of their hearts, rather than just shoving down the injustices often thrust upon us. But, it's *not okay* to shut everyone off because someone else hurt us. In my lifetime there have been so many. "This time/person/situation is different. I can let him/her in because he/she 'gets' it." Nope. Burned. Next time, same thing. So, I do it too. I build the high, concrete walls and hold the bitter grudges because getting hurt sucks! One particular wall is up because of broken promises from the people whom I should've been able to trust. I built another one to keep out people who preyed on my innocence. The next one was to lock out all the users and mistreaters. I constructed another wall to block the noise of unkind words meant to break me down. Pretty soon, I found myself surrounded and alone.

So, I have also humbly realized that it's smart to put a door in your walls. I'm not suggesting that you don't build them, but you just might want the opportunity to open that door sometime. There might be someone you want to let in, so give yourself the option. Make sure it's a wooden door so you can hear them knocking. Also, build a little shelf on your walls on which to hold your little grudges; you can keep them in little labeled jars and see them whenever you want to remind yourself of the things and people to watch out for, but you don't have to harbor them in your heart. But make sure they're glass jars so you can shatter them when you're ready. There's a purpose for protection, and you should absolutely have those mechanisms in place for yourself. No one takes better care of you than you do! I'm just not of the belief anymore that being a solitary prisoner in your walls is such a great plan. We aren't destined for that.

So, the next time I teach the "The Interlopers," and a smart student is there offering up the wisdom, I'll have even more to add.

Mind Your Own Hair Business

Karen Taylor

WE WOMEN SPEND ENTIRELY TOO MUCH time focusing on our outward appearance and not enough time on our inner lives. When I say "our inner lives," I am not necessarily referring to the old adage of "beauty is only skin deep." What I mean is for us to pay attention to our worth as human beings and our inner work or purpose. Appearance is important, and by no means do I intend to give the impression that we shouldn't care about the health of our hair, skin, face, etc. We should, *and* what if our goal is to achieve the appearance we wish to achieve for ourselves and not our culture? What if we show up simply as ourselves? Hair is one of the issues many women struggle with; personally, it has always been one of my main concerns. Our hair is important to us, and that is okay. It can be empowering to find the hair and beauty traits that reflect our authenticity. Authenticity is the name of the game, but this has not been the cultural norm when it comes to hair. I consider myself to have "big hair," and in my own experience, hair has been an outward representation of women fighting for their independence and authenticity.

Both my sister's hair and my hair are thick, coarse, and naturally curly and wavy. I always sought solace that at least one other person, my sister, went through the same hair woes as I did. The lady who has been doing my hair for years asked me why I didn't like to wear mine curly because it was so beautiful. I responded in my normal assertiveness, "Because if I wear it curly, I have to have a lot of product so that it is not frizzy, and that product makes my scalp itch. It is also very hot because no air can get through." What I wanted to add was, "And I hate having hair so big that it looks like someone hit me with a taser." Let me interrogate that for a moment. Why is it that I am so opposed to having big hair? Could it be because I don't want to call undue attention to myself? Is it because I fear being judged by the appearance of my unruly locks? The answer is most likely yes to all three questions, but why is that? Hair struggles for women are not new, I'm afraid.

The roaring '20s brought to bear women known as flappers, who cut their hair into bobs to represent their views on how they wanted to experience freedom in their femaleness. This may seem trivial, yet at that point in history, respectable women were not supposed to cut their hair short, at least that is what many folks thought. So in a way, the bob haircuts were an expression of women asserting their desire for independence. Fast forward to the 1960s, and the hair trends for my sister and I went from the 1950s tall mounds of stiff hair, sprayed in place to long, straight, mostly blonde tresses, the flat look attained by actually ironing the hair on an ironing board. The 70s brought on the "fly-back bangs" sprayed in place so that the entire "wing" could be raised from the head by grabbing one strand of hair and lifting it, resembling a rather oddly shaped bird in flight. The 80s moved into the big hair, and later, by means of Paul Mitchell's and other products, bangs were coated with this holding elixir into a palm-tree looking shock of hair standing straight up from the head. The 80s would've been a good time for my sister and me to take advantage of that big hair, but our hair was just too big and unruly, even for the big-hair 80s. Our frizz, at least to us, was beyond the pale.

If anyone revisits those old photographs and TV shows sporting the big hair trend of the 80s, it will be evident that there were no defrizz products available. The norm was to use stiffening hairspray to hold big tufts of hair. The hair looked deep-fried and resembled a cone of cotton candy from the fair. The tresses screamed for some moisture. That hairspray smelled awful and caused a lot of damage to the ozone. I suspect all that fried hair piercing the air cut wounds in the atmosphere. At any rate, my sister and I tended to use hot rollers and curling irons to tame the wild beast that was our heritage. Like many women have experienced, I was attempting to fit my hair into cultural norms of the time. Even now, despite having no problem asserting my uniqueness and independence as a woman, I still find myself working hard to smooth and tame my locks.

One reason for my consternation regarding my hair has to do with my early years of having big, frizzy hair that didn't resemble the other girls my age. I spent many years trying different cuts to be more acceptable. I would love to be able to say that I no longer do this, but that would be a lie. Unfortunately, I haven't reached the point in my evolution as a woman that I can maneuver through my life without considering the state of my hair.

Throughout our lives, my sister and I have struggled with trying to tame our large and wild tresses, and when we were trying in our teens to tame our mass of frizz and coarseness, there were no flat irons available to us and very little defrizz products. The ones on the market were nowhere near the quality of the ones today. The real question is why is it that we felt our hair was so unacceptable?. To this day, we both spend time smoothing our hair. I wonder if we had been born into a culture that celebrated big, wild, uncontrolled hair, would we have had different personalities. It is hard for me to imagine that, so I don't have the answer, but I suspect we would have. Maybe we would've been more confident, or maybe we would have been arrogant and vain. Perhaps our having different hair texture has been a good thing, a thing to assist us in becoming strong women. It's a mystery worth considering.

Cultural changes didn't really affect my views on my hair, and this is probably because the beauty norms never eliminated smooth hair as the most desirable. Despite the big, fried hair trends of the '80s, long, smooth, flowing locks of shiny beauty never really disappeared from the culture. There were always a couple of famous actresses or models whose hair was the envy of girls like us who just wanted "normal" hair. Think *Baywatch*. Even if my sister and I managed to get our hair relaxed and closer to those *Baywatch* blonde babes' hair, let a drop of rain or a hint of humidity anywhere near a strand of our tresses, and all that work with heat products would go up in floofy, frizzy, flamboyance. Apparently, big frizzy hair wasn't representative of the most desired look for attractiveness in women; just like long, leggy, big-breasted babes with flat stomachs and junk in the trunk held the top standard for beauty. Could it be that big things on women are scary? There has been a trend in our culture to accept beauty in all sizes, but the underlying norm is still small and smooth, for both bodies and hairstyles. There is a poem by Marge Piercy entitled, "Barbie Doll" that I recommend all women read, and if you have a daughter, read it together.

Length became an issue as I grew older. At one point, my hair was halfway down my back, but when I reached 60, I decided it was time to get real. I was tired of having to spend so much time trying to keep my curls under control, so I decided to get it cut to shoulder length and layered to take the weight off and reduce blow drying time. By doing this, I reduced the amount of curls I had because I have a long curl pattern. I was happy with this "cooler" version of hair; any woman close to my age knows about the heat attacks from hormonal fluctuations induced by menopause. I also decided to stop coloring my hair and go gray. I am glad I did because my hair also grows pretty quickly, and the touch up on the roots was rather frequent, and I was getting tired of dealing with it. I also feel this was a rather spiritual choice because I decided it was time to be who I am and not concern myself with aging and trying to cover things like gray and wrinkles because they happen, and that is life. That is the lesson I've learned regarding my hair and my appearance. I just wish I had learned it earlier.

Now that I am in my 60s, I can feel the social pressure for older women to wear their hair short. I've heard that a lot over the years and have often wondered why that is a thing. I've also heard that women over 50 shouldn't wear their hair past their collar bone. I wonder if that is due to the strong cultural belief that youth is the only venue of beauty and long hair is a symbol of said beauty only afforded to the "young." Such tropes demonstrate the stereotypes women often operate in, many of us doing so unconsciously. Could the answers to some of these things be that women's power, like Samson from the Old Testament of the Bible, is encased in their hair? It certainly causes some pontification; that's for sure. I think women do attribute much of their power to their hair and other physical attributes. For better or worse, to this day, some women still attribute their self-worth and value to their hairstyle, waist size, and how young they look.

I am fortunate to have healthy, thick hair, and I make sure I send forth my gratitude for that. I would prefer that I didn't have to deal with the coarseness and frizziness, but I work with my hair now rather than fighting it into submission thanks to hair appliances and smoothing products. I have to learn to take the advantages with the disadvantages, and really, if I think about it, the only reason my sister and I felt we had to struggle with trying to tame our hair is because our hair didn't fit into the accepted beauty standards of our culture. I would like to say that things have changed, and perhaps to some degree they have, but fashion and fads still dictate the choices of many. I would venture to say that many women still attempt to follow fashion and beauty trends. I still follow some myself, I suppose, but I am not as susceptible as I once was. That has come with age and wisdom. We should be able to be ourselves and wear our hair as we choose and not feel less than because our attributes are different from the accepted norms.

So, big hair, big curly hair, smooth hair, short hair, long hair, no hair, it doesn't matter what we choose, so long as we choose it for ourselves and not according to a standard of beauty set by a culture that is outside of ourselves. Let's dress and groom ourselves in a fashion that makes us happy with ourselves and where we are in our lives. If that means we choose to color or not color, flat iron or not flat iron, gray or pink, the choice can reflect who we truly are as women and human beings.

Issues

Tonya Reid

Isn't It Enough that they Inherit our hips and medical histories?

I was raised by a single mother who worked her ass off at a bank. She was always the first one there and the last one to leave. Trying to make ends meet did not afford her the luxury of coming to eat lunch with me or chaperoning field trips or being a coveted Grade Mother when I was growing up.

I decided when I had my son Porter that I wasn't going to miss out on A THING! I've experienced more than the average trips to petting zoos, hayrides, corn mazes, classroom parties, loud, sticky bus rides where I mentally prepare a list of teachers to nominate for sainthood, and Chick-fil-A lunches shared while perched on an elementary school stool no bigger than a chicken nugget. If a driver was needed for a field trip or an extra hand holder was required for a stroll downtown to a museum, I was The Mama Bear Extraordinaire!

I've always been amazed how parenthood affords us an opportunity to do things AGAIN for the FIRST time through our children's eyes. How truly healing parenting can be to our own inner child. I also know that the minute you think, "Hey! I got this!" is the moment you realize you don't have a frigging clue!

One of my biggest AHA parenting moments happened when Porter was 4 or 5, and he attended the Charlotte Montessori

School. They announced that swimming lessons were going to be offered, and they needed several parents to transport the kids to the local aquatic center. I happily moved my work schedule around to accommodate and relished in being able to do so. Chaperoning meant meeting at the school, filling my car with as many kids and their booster seats as safely possible, helping them change into their swimsuits in the locker room before the lessons and back into dry clothes after, watching everyone from the side of the pool in 153% humidity where my pores expanded larger than my pupils and my hair wondered why I even bothered, then hauling everyone back to school.

The director of the school was an energetic man named Bill. He always drove a few students so he could spend the class time swimming laps in the big pool. The school secretary was a woman named Pat, who I suspect spent most of her time managing Bill.

On one particular day about 4 weeks into lessons, I pulled into the parking lot at the school. Bill was leading the charge frantically corralling the kids, busting a move to the cars that weren't there yet, while Pat was yelling out the door that it wasn't time to go. I saw my child in the middle of the pack, head thrown back, mouth open wide, wailing with all of his might, the drawstring to his bag clutched in his tiny hand and the filled to the gills contents dragging along behind him. My maternal instincts went into overdrive, and I threw my SUV into park. I checked the clock on my dash and saw that I was early.

I was flooded with memories from my childhood. My own father who ironically was named Bill was never anywhere to be found, and when he did show up, it was always a couple of hours after the fact. And my mother, you guessed it, also named Pat… I swear you can't make this shit up… always managing the people at work, leaving me the last to be picked up.

I dashed across the lot, bent down to console Porter and exclaimed, "Sweetheart! I'm here! Mommy is here! Oh Baby, did you think I wasn't coming?"

Porter immediately righted himself and looked at me confused. He said, "Huh? What? No, Mom. I knew you were coming. I just don't want to go swimming."

It was a neon 2x4 revelation from the Universe! I love when the lessons are comically crystal clear. Wow! Our lessons are our lessons and our children's lessons are theirs to learn. And isn't that divine by design? Isn't it enough that they inherit our hips and our medical histories?

I

Just Don't Leave Me Behind

Tonya Reid

LADY IN THE VAN.

Several years ago, my best friend Shelly shared an experience she had that has not only stuck with me, it seems to take on a deeper personal meaning with each passing year. I have her permission to share here under one condition … as long as I DON'T say that SHE is the lady in the van! Cuz nobody wants to be the lady in the van! Let me explain.

Shelly and her college buddies graduated from NC State in 1990 ready to make their mark on the world. These eight women pledged to get together at least once a year for a beach weekend and still honor that promise some 30+ yrs later.

On a trip about 20 years ago, Shelly and one of her friends were road tripping together for 4 hours to the coast. They were riding along, chit chatting, and catching up with each other's lives. Traffic was heavy, and they found themselves inching along next to the same cars over and over, jockeying for positions ahead, behind or stopped next to another car.

The same minivan seemed to be tethered to their every move for 30 minutes or so. The conversation switched to mini van yay or nay? I don't know about her friend, but I KNOW Shelly isn't a minivan mama. She's more the SUV type.

The women started noticing other things about the van and its inhabitants.

The mom looked exhausted. The kids looked perfectly rested, albeit a bit bored. Oh how delicious would 15 minutes of boredom feel for that lady?

The kids all had on spiffy outfits and fresh haircuts. The Van Ma'am looked disheveled from top to window level, suggesting the rest wasn't much better. When was the last time this lady had one moment of self-care? And, no, waiting for everyone to get their shit in the car doesn't count.

The kids all looked athletic and fit with their myriad of equipment stuffed in the back. The unpaid maternal Uber driver looked like 8 years later she still had 10 lbs of baby weight to shed for each of her three kids. Good Lord, can she even go for a walk after dropping the kids off at activities? Nope, bet she runs the concession stand!

All of this really hit home for Shelly and her buddy. They were in the throes of parenting themselves. This lady was like catching a glimpse of yourself in a department store mirror. You know the ones! The three-way ones! When you see your back end and your sides you say "Where did I go?" or "Who traded necks with me while I was asleep last night?" or "Whose ass is THAT?"

They rolled into the rental determined. Over cocktails that night, they recounted the trip and the impact of witnessing their caregiving comrade. They made the first ever, or that I've heard of, Lady in the Van Pledge. If any of them became that woman, they'd be ripped from their environment and whisked off to the salon, a walk around the block, and a fresh change of clothes. If it looked more like the world was leaving its mark on them, an intervention would be imminent!

No mom would be left behind.

Kindred

Taylor Edwards

MY HOME WAS BUILT IN THE late 1800s.
Parts of it, anyway.
Generations of Southern Baptists,
Men that were called preachers,
Good men,
Powerful men,
Women that were called whores,
Difficult women,
Crazy women,
Made their home in this home,

I am of these men and women.

Women that nursed babies,
And rocked the *very big emotions* that raged their little bodies,
Men that saw the sin of the world,
And felt it in their bones,
As they tried really, really hard to shield themselves, their
    women, and their little babies' bodies from it.

I am of these men and women.
So, indeed, this is home—parts of it, anyway.

This home has seen shame and persecution, and these
　　walls have held secret desires and wants and needs
That were oh-too-big for the world they were in.

A century ago, the men and women in this home pushed that
Which only filled their dreams
Down, down, down,
Into the fibers of their DNA and
Shunned that which they wanted
Opting for that which they *should do.*

A century later, I have made this home different.

Where once there were the commandments of a Lord painted to be
hellfire, brimstone, fury, and punishment
There is now psalms that hold incantations
　　of the Feminine Divine, a
softness—in—Her—strength ,
　　accepting—those—who—yearn—to—grow, Goddess
Whose Image I Am Modeled After

Where once there were rods and hickory sticks,
　　branches used as tools to teach
punishment, retribution, obedience,
There are now pages and pages of words daring the
　　holder to break the bonds that have held
growth, home, self, awareness, alignment
*How do you want to show up in the world? How can your hands mold
　　your reality into that for which you want to be, see, know, and love?*

The men and women once in this home worked
And pushed
And planned
And *fit*

So that I could expand-simmer-dream-hope-*be*.

I can't break the generational trauma
Without first
Thanking that which
Got
Me
Here

Thank you to those men and women.
May your bones rest in peace
And spirit and soul dance
Around
Desires Reclaimed.

K

Letter to Brooke

Tonya Reid

A FRIEND'S DAUGHTER GOT MARRIED A few years ago, and another friend asked all of us old, married ladies to jot down advice to have bound in a book as a wedding present. Here was mine.

Brooke,

You know I have my PhD in human behavior from being a hairdresser for 30 years. So I am going to impart the wisdom I have gained about marriage during that time. First of all, marriage was a good idea about 150 years ago when the bride was 15, the groom was 35, and life expectancy was 42. The guy would get the farm going, give you six kids to work it, and be dead in 7 years. Come on! You can endure anything for 7 years. Easy peasy. Well, modern medicine screwed that up, so here's what I suggest...

1. There's being right, and there's being happy. Sometimes (let's be honest, most of the time) you'll be right, but always choose to be happy.
2. Take time for what I call "remembering what color eyes each other have" by going on dates BEFORE you want to gouge each other's eyes out.
3. You may not believe this now, but you'll get to the point that you find everything wrong with Alex. You may try to change

him. You may try counseling. At that point, try just LOVING HIM. A little love goes a long way.

4. Lastly, if none of this works for you and you want to chop him up and bury him in the backyard, I'll be there for you, shovel in hand, no questions asked.

Good Luck and Much Love,
Tonya

Moving on from Mother

Kristin Bowen

Trigger Warning: This piece speaks to issues of suicidal ideation.

IT HAS BEEN OVER 30 YEARS that I've been mourning the loss of the mother I never had, a mother, quite frankly, I never will have. There are times I daydream about what it could be like to have a close bond together. Brunch on the weekends, daily phone calls to check in and say, "hi" or tell her about the kids, calling to ask for advice and to hear some of her wisdom. In my mind, we would take impromptu trips to the grocery store together as we buy the ingredients to her famous recipe. That is never going to happen for us. There is no brunch, no happy phone calls, and certainly not a recipe we are cooking together. I still yearn for the day that I'll see her and run straight into her arms and collapse, knowing I'm safe and secure. That day isn't going to come either. What does it feel like to call out to your mom for help when the kids are running wild, your car breaks down, or you aren't sure if you're going to make rent that month? Do daughters actually call their moms when they go through a break up or have a disagreement with a friend? Not me.

A Letter to My Mother

It's taken me a very long time to write this letter. I hope you understand this has not come easy, and I don't take it lightly. It may be time to "call it quits." For God's sake, Mom, we've been struggling with this relationship for years. It's clear to me we both want something we have never had, a mother that cares for us so deeply that she wraps us in her arms, protecting us from the cruel, cold world. A mother that squeezes us so tight that we can't help but feel the love radiating out of her body and into our own. The type of mom that loves us unconditionally through every vein in her body, without boundaries, never giving up or losing hope. I know you have seen the shows on TV with moms who bake cookies with their daughters on Sunday afternoons and get pedicures together. The kind of mom that giggles and laughs with their daughter about childhood memories of getting a bead stuck up their nose or the first time the kid accidentally said a curse word. The ones who bond with the daughter over the way Dad fell asleep on the couch snoring so loud that it could have woken the neighbors? That kind of mom. We don't have that relationship, and that's alright.

I get it mom; you don't know how to give this kind of love, and I don't blame you. I had to teach myself as well. Maybe you've never received it yourself. You don't have an example of what it looks like. Where do we go from here? How do we save our sanity? How do we repair our future and stop the generational trauma of over-stimulated mothers who resent their daughters? I'm not sure how to fix US, but I do know what I can do for myself. I can't be silent any longer. I can't continue to hold my words inside. It's my time to be heard. So here I stand, sharing all the things I wish had been done differently. It's the only way to stop myself from repeating these actions with my own children. You can hear them from my point of view with empathy and understanding or choose to be hurt by them. I say this with conviction, knowing that we are in control of our own emotions. Know that my words aren't meant to be harsh or damaging, though my truth may, indeed, cut you to the core. I expect nothing in return and only hope for the ability to be understood, or at the very least, for my words to be said out loud as I sit in my truth.

I'm grieving the loss of a mother I never had a chance of receiving. When I reframe the situation, and look back at my life from another point of view, I can actually find gratitude in how I was raised. It may, in fact, be part of my superpowers and what drives my purpose today. Would I be the same strong, resourceful, flexible, and loving person if things had gone differently? I can be grateful for these traits and the ability to learn and grow from my own experiences. As I work towards acceptance of where we are, it's only fair that you know the pain I have endured so that you can begin to accept our relationship and my perspective as well, that is if you choose to accept it.

As a child, I always felt as though I was taking care of you emotionally, making sure we stayed safe. Safe from physical harm, psychological warfare, and emotional distress. I remember consoling you when you were upset, wrapping my arms around you tightly, caressing your hair and reminding you everything would be okay. Yet, I couldn't find your arms when I was the one who needed the consoling. There were a lot of dramatic times in our lives when I was young, and it was constant chaos, from the constant moving and new places to lay my head each year to abusive boyfriends who yelled, screamed, and disciplined me in ways I could never imagine subjecting my own kids to now. You often seemed closed off and emotionally unavailable. Looking back, I kept quite a bit of my emotions and depression to myself (thus the reason for the attempted suicides at such a young age). I saw myself as the problem. If I could simply disappear, perhaps it would make everything better for everyone, and I would get to escape the constant torture and pain of living. I didn't feel like I had anyone who was supporting me, nobody I could rely on 100% if I needed to talk or cry or kick and scream. It felt like a conditional love that could only be accessed if I did the "right" thing (made sure the lights were turned off, did all my chores perfectly, didn't talk back, and got good grades in school). I resented you for not keeping me safe. By the time I moved in with my dad, I no longer needed anybody. I was confident that I could take care of myself because I had already been doing it for so long. Even then, you were angry with me. I suppose you felt abandoned, or as though I was ungrateful. Maybe it sparked some unresolved childhood trauma that triggered an unfavorable response. I did not sense any fear or worry for my safety on your part, only disappointment because I refused to remain in your control.

I could go on and on about examples of how you let me down or things that make me upset with how you treated me, but I don't think it would be helpful. I could discuss the time you accused me of stealing money or moved halfway across the country when I was a new, single mom trying to find my way. Maybe I should tell you about the ways you have disrespected my house by putting your shoes on the furniture or keeping the front door wide open in the winter, even though you would have smacked me across the face as a child for doing something that bold. Would it help if I tried to explain how your attempts at being involved in my life have become more of a burden than a blessing as I am required to answer constant questions and rearrange my schedule to squeeze you in? Perhaps the most impactful reason that I have kept you at arms length is because I cannot trust you to keep me safe. I never could. If you think back to the times I've questioned you about my childhood, you already know this. You know what happened, and you never did anything about it. I have forgiven you, but I cannot forget.

* * *

Therapists Office

"What would you say to her if she were sitting right in front of you, right now?" said my hypnotherapist. I had paid over $1,000 and planned to spend 12 consecutive weeks with this person to change my life. It seemed like a pivotal moment, yet my mind was blank. All this time and money to overcome the pain, trauma, and resentment I experienced with my mother. Mother, that feels like a harsh name to call the person who carried you in her womb, wiped away your tears, and held you in her arms. I tried working through the pain on my own, even pretended parts of my life never happened just so I could forget. However, you can't forget the things I saw and experienced.

So here I was, with a damn hypnotherapist, trying to trick myself, will myself to just get over it. We had gone through several weeks of mental exercises and repetitive sayings, tapping parts of my body to make the lessons stick and unraveling the parts of my life that felt icky but also comfortable and warm. They were parts of me, part of my story, and the reason I am the person I am today. This was our tenth session together. It was time for me to visualize an empty, round room, sort of like a dome with white walls. In my mind, it was sterile and almost like one of those robot or spaceship movies where the walls are clean and secure. It seemed to me like an interrogation room. I mentally placed two chairs in the middle of the room, also white, no screws. Imagine those IKEA chairs that are super smooth and durable. They don't look comfortable to the naked eye but are surprisingly cozy. So I took a seat in one of the chairs. Strangely, in my mind, I could see myself, but it was also like I was viewing the back of my head. I was able to toggle between different views, like I was playing a race car video game where you can switch between being in the driver's seat, viewing the back of your car, or being all the way up at the front view and not seeing anything around or behind you. The therapist's voice was soothing and calm. She asked me to take a moment to visualize the person who I felt caused the most trauma in my life. Immediately, my stomach got tight, and my throat closed up. I knew everyone who was coming into this room with me. She encouraged me to picture every tiny detail of each person from their fingernails to their hairstyles, the clothes they would be wearing, their mannerisms, and the sounds of their voices. This was to be as real as possible. So one by one, I ushered in each of the people who caused me harm I pulled in everyone from ex boyfriends to my dad and even some high school friends. I knew there was one more person that I hadn't summoned to the room yet. Was I even ready to do this? Just the pure thought of pulling her into an imaginary room gave me anxiety and a knot in my stomach. I did it anyway. We had gotten to this point, and I wasn't willing to turn back now. I "invited" my mother into the bright white room and had her sit in the chair directly across from me. My hypnotherapist asked, "What do you want to say to her right now?" My words came out choppy. I still had that lump in my throat. My mind was blank. Then, the only thing I could muster was, "You fucking bitch!" over and over and over again. "You fucking bitch!" I said repeatedly. I whispered the damning words out loud to her as they trembled across my lips. She may hold them against me, even in this imaginary room that she didn't know existed. The therapist asked me to speak with more emotion, to be bold. Didn't she know it was exhausting just to drag the words from the pit of my stomach and up to my throat, let alone scream them with the full range of emotion that they held?! I wanted to shout, stomp my feet, and bang my fists. I wanted to purge the memories, the feelings, all of the pain I had ever felt and let it burst out of my body, but I just couldn't get the courage. It was like she, my mother, was still in front of me in real life.

Have you ever seen *The Lion King*? It reminds me of the time when Simba is asked to roar. He stands up straight with all the confidence in the world, pushes his shoulders back and takes a deep breath. He thinks he is ready to let out the roar of his life, and then, out comes a tiny, squeaky meow. That's exactly how I felt in this moment; a small part of me was liberated that I took the first baby step towards healing, and another part of me was devastated with embarrassment and confusion. Why couldn't I just say it? Just scream it? She wasn't even there. She wouldn't even know!

* * *

I've gone through many stages of this little dance of trauma—denial, avoidance, grief, sadness, anger and even rebellion. Now, I keep the water running the whole time I brush my teeth, not because I'm wasteful or don't care about the environment. I do it to get on her nerves, and she isn't even there. It's my tiny act of rebellion, a punch in the gut simply because I know she would disapprove. I embrace my kids a little tighter, spoil them a little more, hug and kiss them twice as much as I ever thought I would because these are the things I wish I had growing up. So I rebel. I go to all their games and know all of their friends. I make sure not to wear tight or revealing clothing, don't place myself in the spotlight or draw attention to myself when their friends are around, all in the name of avoiding second hand embarrassment for my children. I refuse to compete with them or outshine them because I think it is my job to put them on a pedestal and uplift them like nobody else. I would certainly never wear white to their wedding, prance around in their favorite jeans while they were 19 and pregnant, or abandon them in a foreign country because they attempted to set boundaries and I continued to break them.

And here we are, all that pain and suffering and nobody wins. I've decided it's time for peace and forgiveness. I have been called to end this cycle and release this extra baggage so that I can grow and give space for my children to heal from this trauma too.

The truth is, or perhaps I should clarify, my truth is, most people don't know my mom. I'm not sure she even knows herself. Hell, do any of us really take the time to look at the deep, dark places within ourselves? And what if her deep dark places were caused by somebody else's trauma and pain that they didn't know what to do with, so they dumped it on her? I'm not making excuses, believe me. I've placed a ton of guilt and blame on her for every single part of my childhood and a good chunk of my adult life too. There is a tumultuous and complicated relationship that lies beneath the surface between my mother and I. My entire childhood, I unknowingly played the role of mother, protector, and caretaker. My mother, on the other hand, was the one I was taking care of, both physically,spiritually, and emotionally. So who was taking care of me? Nobody prepared me for nights consoling her on the kitchen floor, rubbing her back and wiping tears, after an abusive boyfriend (one of many) threw a plate of spaghetti against the wall. Nobody told me as I got older, I would have to be the responsible one managing and lending money to her in order to pay the household bills. Did anybody tell me that I would have to dim myself down, be a "good girl" and avoid trouble at all costs so that she wouldn't have to deal with any more stress? Maybe I didn't need the warning. Maybe I have held onto this pain for so long because it has become a badge of honor, proof that I survived hell. And maybe it just doesn't feel fair to be the one taking care of everybody else when no one is taking care of you, not in the ways that you need any way. There are times this pain is just too heavy, yet I carry it around with me every day. And then some days, I want someone else to pick up this baggage and carry it for me. But right now, today, I'm ready to unpack the bags and remove the baggage from my life.

Normalizing
the Unconventional

Amanda Soesbee Kent

ACCORDING TO THE ALL-KNOWING GOOGLE, THERE are 3.8 billion women in this wide world, most of whom started their lives as little girls. "Sweet, innocent, fluffy, [little] girls with rings on their fingers and bells on their toes and a bone in their nose, ho-ho." (Thanks for that, Mother Goose or Ray Stevens, depending on how you were raised.) More sugar than spice, mostly everything nice. Blonde curls or black braids, roly-poly thighs, baby blue or big brown eyes, glowing cheeks… can you see her? This little impressionable girl who will eventually have to make her own way in the world, one where she is outnumbered by men and undervalued by society. This world will dump expectations on her before she even learns the meaning of the word. It will categorize her, slide her right into her place. And if she stays there, in her lane where she belongs, the arms of the world will embrace and love on her like the princess she is. She'll grow up to be a cheerleader, or maybe a lacrosse star. She'll get an academic scholarship and work a little part time job at the coffee shop. She'll love fashion; she'll wear strawberry lip gloss. She'll join her Mama's sorority and be the apple of her Daddy's eye as he waltzes her down the aisle. She'll dress her kids in matching, monogrammed, seersucker jumpers and make a killer pot roast. And that's great—good for her! It's a wonderful life that she has.

But what if she doesn't? Or she isn't? She can't. I'm not. I can't. I am she, the one who doesn't fit.

And from what I'm learning, there are 3,799,799,799 little girls who need to know that it is okay NOT to fit.

My mom and dad met in college. They attended Erskine because they're good, little Reformed Presbyterians and did what their parents wanted. Mom, probably because she spent her childhood raising her three younger brothers, played intramural football; Dad was the coach. "Give the ball to that girl who can run!" 50+ years later, they're still runnin' (perhaps trippin' over each other along the way), and here we are. Dad continued to coach all the sports, leading soccer and football teams to championships. Even in her 70s, Mom is lean and fit and would probably water-ski daily if her hands would allow. Nana, Mama Lou, and Aunt Sara Jo? Basketball. Uncles? Baseball and football. My younger brother is an excellent all-around athlete who married a state champion softball player. They both still play a co-ed softball game every now and then when he isn't on a field coaching my nephews. Every single family member…athlete. Me? Can't catch a cold with both hands. The only thing I can throw is a fit. Or my scale across the room as it continually reminds me how unathletic of a stature I possess.

Yeah, but sports is just one thing, you say. So let's look from another angle. I'm the first grandchild on both sides and the oldest of the cousins. All eyes on me, the first to do everything. Except, nope! Thank goodness the four or five in line after me did it right. Went to school, met a nice girl/boy, got married, had kids. Picket fences, mini-vans, and mortgages, oh my! Me? Not a mom. Not a wife until almost age (*gasp*) 50. Instead of sorority soirees and bachelorette bashes in my 20s, I was too busy falling in love with education, exploring the world, and wooing myself. I'm a terrible housekeeper and a barely average cook. Even now, I'd much prefer to eat every meal out and use my kitchen purely for sweater storage like my *Sex and the City* idol, Carrie Bradshaw, did.

Make no mistake, I love my family for better and for worse with all my heart. I love my cousins, who are more like friends, and I simply adore their kids. I love that we all live within hollerin' distance from each other. I love going to everyone's games and matches, wearing the colors and cheering for the teams. I cherish every single memory of their weddings, their baby showers. I have never been purposefully made to feel left out.

But I was, and still am, left out. What do you do with someone like me, someone who ought to be "a normal girl" and just…isn't?

I don't fit, literally and figuratively. Sadly, struggling through the molasses of my teens and 20s (yeah, yeah… and my 30s), it took me almost 4 decades to realize that IT. IS. OKAY.

I am a large woman with a large voice and large ideas. I used to care what others might think about that, and it used to worry me to the point of eating disorders that I was the gray sheep of the family. Yes, my parents are proud of me and love me very much. Yes, my mother always said, "Remember who you are and whose you are." But I was always so torn! Who am I?? How do I fit?? Am I Daddy's Little Girl? No. Am I Mommy's Mini-Me? No. I'm a good musician, but not an athlete. Academic, but not top of the class. Average at this, not exceptional at that. Tried too hard to be normal, didn't try hard enough to fit in. Third wheel in every friend group, single girl at the dance. I couldn't please my Dad. I couldn't follow my Mom's ways of keeping her mouth shut to maintain peace. Against my teacher-parents' wishes, all I ever wanted to be was a teacher. My Nana, God rest her sweet soul, was worried until her death day that I wouldn't have a man to take care of me.

Why did no one tell me? Why did no one tell me that I didn't need that man or that softball glove, that luxurious straight hair or that shiny blue ribbon to be a whole, complete young woman? Why didn't I hear that I was as beautiful as my teeny tiny friends were, that I shouldn't worry about the talents I don't have, and that I should punch someone in the face the next time they told me, "Don't worry; your time is coming," at a wedding?! (Maybe I should've said that same thing to them at a funeral...)

And more importantly, since no one showed me the way, how did I get from there to here?

There, it's "We might as well call you Thunder Thighs," and "My daughter is Dolly Parton already, at age 13," and "Nobody cares about band concerts, Amanda." There, you hear "Why aren't you married yet?" and "Don't you want kids?" and "You are coming to church, right?" There, you change yourself constantly to be whoever the other person—your parent, your teacher, your peer, your boyfriend—wants you to be. You pretend. You give up things that really matter to you, because you think that doing so will create the happiness you seek.

But HERE. Here is a sigh of relief, a place of acceptance and forgiveness. Here, we say "I don't have to go to a church to be a Christian," and "My best friend is a gay man, and he will be my man-of-honor," and "Yes, Queen, you rock those curves!" (Thank you, Lizzo.) Here, you drink whiskey with your sushi and wear Crocs with your Michael Kors jeans and ask for zero-turn lawn mowers for Christmas. (I got one. Her name is Martha.) Here, you ignore the people who are amazed that you aren't a mom who's been divorced multiple times, or who look at you condescendingly on the beach because you refuse to cover up. Here, you get college degrees because you want them, not because someone wants you to have them. You spend your free time reading Stephen King books even though your house is filthy. You sleep too late, you drink too much, you still eat Fruity Pebbles, and you'd rather visit Italy and Ireland than save for retirement. You and Martha mow your own damn grass! When you finally choose to fall in love, it's with an introverted, divorced father who doesn't drink coffee or alcohol and who plays video games. Literally your total opposite. You've learned that the people who judge you, even if they matter to you, don't control you.

Ladies, girls, sweet princesses, you will love it here! It's the best place. Will you be lonely? Yep. Will it feel wrong at first, to turn away from all that "normal?" Absolutely. It will feel like you've abandoned your dream until you realize that it wasn't really your dream to begin with. It will feel like you've wasted years being "not you." And maybe you did. It's okay, I wasted 30+! Being here will not stop the people from judging. They will still have passive aggressive comments. "You know the service starts at 5pm, right?" "Don't you want to save that money for a rainy day?" "I don't care what size you are just as long as you're healthy." "People your age still play beer pong?" And furthermore, there's no GPS to get you here. No map, no arrow, no tour guide. If you don't find **HERE** all by yourself, then you didn't arrive. But that's why I'm telling you it's okay to pack your bags and **GO**. Leave behind the voices who say wonderfully nice things that simply aren't what you want. Leave behind the ideals; they belong to someone else. Want the carefree, love the unenviable, achieve the unconventional!

Get **HERE** as fast as you can.

And if it matters to you that much, buy your own damn trophies! Who needs sports anyway?

That Old Time Religion

Melisa Graham

MY GRANDMOTHER AND GRANDFATHER DIDN'T GET along. I didn't like him all that much either. He was, in my opinion, bombastic and mean. He earned his living as a mechanic and spent his spare time as a Southern Baptist preacher in a small, country church. His every sermon was fire and brimstone and the wrath of the Old Testament God. Some might say he was charismatic—a smooth talker, a handsome man with a ready smile and a joke for every stranger he met. To me, he was the man who pinched me and spoke gruffly when I was in his way, who spoke to my grandmother like she was his maid.

From my earliest days, she was constantly saying things like, "When you start school, I'm leaving that man," "When you get to middle school, I'm leaving that man," "When you get your driver's license, I'm leaving that man," … and on she went, constantly moving the needle until it was too late. Divorce is a sin, after all.

In her later years, she confessed that he was something of a player as a young man (a "fuckboy" as the kids say now). One day she came home with an armload of groceries and babies to find him in bed with two women. Two. In the 1940s. My grandfather "found God" soon after that tryst and went to Fruitland Baptist Bible College to become an ordained minister. I imagine my grandmother's fire and brimstone had something to do with it. Or maybe she brought out the pistol to help him come to Jesus.

Fortunately, my parents didn't subject my siblings and me to membership in my grandfather's church. No, we went to the Church of the Nazarene. It was a similar brand of fundamentalist evangelical Christianity, except the preacher didn't yell. Neither did the congregants, although they frequently interrupted the sermon to "witness," to tell the whole gathering how God had worked in their lives that week. The Nazarene church also had music, which I loved, but they frowned upon dancing. Swaying and clapping was okay though, apparently, because that happened at every revival service when a guest musical group was brought in to renew our faith (and fill the collection plates).

We went to church twice on Sundays (thrice if you count Sunday School) and at least once during the week. The weekday visit started with getting dragged along with my mom to Wednesday night Bible study, but somewhere in there, I got talked into the Bible quiz team and had my own weekly appointment with the Word.

Bible quizzing was my jam for a while. Winning recipe: take a book nerd with low self-esteem and ask her multiple-choice questions about a single book in the Bible for months on end in competition with kids from other churches. It spoke both to my primary interest—reading anything I could get my hands on—and to my primary neurosis—proving to myself and others that I had value in this world. I rarely missed, and when I did, it was because the question was phrased oddly to throw us off. Those weekly quizzes were probably what inspired me to read the Bible, the whole thing. I wanted to be one of those people who could whip out a Bible verse for any situation, recite any chapter and verse on a dime. I ran into two big problems in this endeavor: one, my memory wasn't quite that good, even back then when it was so much better than it is now; two, the more I read the Bible, the more confused I became. The thing doesn't make any sense. It contradicts itself at every turn, and parts of it make God sound downright evil. It's almost as if it were never meant to be a single book taken by its readers to be the infallible word of God, I would have thought my little girl brain could have worked its way around the cognitive dissonance.

I'd always been frightened by tales from the Old Testament in our Sunday School classes, but I tried my best to be a good girl. I tried to absorb the messages the Sunday School teacher said was behind them: Eve screwed us all when she ate that damn apple (I'm paraphrasing of course); God is not a vegetarian, and we are our brothers' keepers; Abraham was a righteous man because he followed God's commands no matter what; the world needed a clean start with Noah and his family, the only righteous people left on the whole face of the earth, and a breeding pair of every single animal, bird, and insect on land (the fishes would be fine, but no one could tell me how the plants survived); and so on.

I simply had to trust that if God told my dad to sacrifice me, well then, it was part of God's plan. I focused on the notion of cute and fuzzy animals marching two by two onto Noah's Ark and snuggling into their stalls. I dismissed any logic that told me Noah's grandkids would've looked like tasty snacks to the lions and alligators. I stared at the picture-book images of a smooth, unblemished water world and burned them into my mind. When my imagination tried to draw a violent wall of water sweeping away mommies and babies, I ripped those crayons from my mental talons and melted them in holy fire.

When you put those scary stories into the context of religion, they're even worse because they're not alone: they come packaged with doctrine and dogma and layer upon layer of flawed human lenses. I won't describe the many aspects of Christianity that are not biblical since hundreds of books have been written about it. I'll just share what one of my childhood church leaders told me: "That which does not directly glorify God glorifies Satan."

For the first few decades of my life, I figured I was most definitely hell bound, and there was little I could do about it. It was impossible to ask for forgiveness for every single little sin I committed, for all the ways I might have inadvertently hurt someone, for all the times I didn't glorify God in my every word and deed. I remember believing as early as 4 years old that I was simply too flawed to hope for salvation. The best I could do was try to be good and appreciate my time on earth.

Somewhere along the way I rebelled. I started picking and choosing the aspects of my religion that I wanted to keep and those I wanted to discard. The curse of Ham? Trash. The earth is 5,000 years old? Trash. Eve's choice to consume knowledge was a sin? Lot was a righteous man and not the worst father ever? Being Christian meant you were good and others were bad? Any literal interpretation of the Bible? Trash, trash, trash, trash. Of course, discarding fundamentalism is easier said than done, particularly for someone who tends toward literal thinking. Once fear moves in, kicking that motherfucker out is a beast—the Beast, if you will.

I did get to keep some lovely things though. The music sticks with me. "Amazing Grace" and "Blessed Assurance" give me chills every time. Some of my father's views stick as well. While on a rare one-on-one outing with him, we passed a scruffy-looking hitchhiker. I asked him why anyone would ever pick up a hitchhiker. He answered that the Bible is full of angels appearing to people as men in need, so we had to treat everyone as if they might be an angel in disguise, with respect and kindness and a helping hand when needed. Mind you, I'm not going to pick up hitchhikers because I don't want to risk being raped and murdered, but I do my best on the respect and kindness part.

When I got to college, I found myself taking mostly English classes with religious themes and religion classes with literary themes, so I double majored in English and religion. I didn't graduate with many marketable skills, but I definitely healed some religious trauma and began cobbling together a new spiritual foundation.

I was invited to read the Bible as a work of literature and discovered the apocryphal gospels. It was life changing. That moment in John 20:16 when Mary Magdalene is grieving alone outside Jesus's tomb is one of my favorite scenes in all of literature, and now I see it copied in every trashy romance I've ever read. She's clearly grieving, and two angel sidekicks appear and pull this "woman, why are you crying" crap. She tells them off and turns around to leave, but a man is standing in her way. He, too, asks why she's crying, but in a softer, actually concerned way. She asks him what he's done with her man. "Mary," he answers so softly, and she realizes it's Jesus! It's like Clark Kent just pulled off his glasses and said, "Lois." Don't get me started on the gorgeous poetry of the Psalms or the pedantic letter-writing skills of Paul (fuck that guy).

In one of my classes, I read an excerpt from the Upanishads, sacred Hindu texts, that said Truth (with a capital T) reveals itself to people in ways they can understand it, resulting in many truths. I have come back to that idea in every season of my life since then. It explained so much to me about religion and people and our varied perspectives on everything.

Around that same time, I learned that both you and I might look at the sky and call it blue, but how your eyes actually see blue might be completely different from how I see blue. My blue might be your red and vice versa. We have no way of knowing someone else's exact lived experience. We can do our best to communicate in words, pictures, music, and art, but ultimately they're all insufficient.

We each stand in a slightly different spot gazing upon Truth—upon God or whatever you want to call it—and trying to understand it from our limited perspectives. The truths we render are mere foretastes of glory divine.

I'll end on this last little hilarious bit—hilarious in a really dark way—I also got married in college. To a man just like my grandfather. Well, he was an atheist, but just like him in every other way that mattered: handsome, charismatic, bit of a fuckboy, considered household chores my domain, got furious if I "told" him to do something instead of asking nicely … you know the type. But, whoa, was I smitten. He transferred into the college down the road from mine. We wanted to live together halfway between, but my parents would never allow us to live in sin. So we had to get married. See? Hilarious.

We were married for 14 years and had two beautiful children. Then my grandmother died. I saw myself going down the same path she did, telling myself I'd leave that man when the kids are older, he gets a new job, I get a new job, he's mentally stable, I'm mentally stable… and ultimately staying right where I was because divorce was wrong. It was, in my mind, the highest magnitude of failure.

Enough. I left him later that year, and in that exodus, I shed something I didn't even realize I'd been dragging around: the tattered remnants of a scared little girl who just wanted to be good.

Period Is Just the Beginning

Rachel Patterson

UGH! PERIOD AGAIN!

This thing called womanhood.
What was never said, but known by most
Tolerable days, in bed for days.
What to do next?
The horrible bending over pain.
Gripping your gut pain.

Not looking forward to that 1 week out of 28 to 32 days.
Going to school grumpy, irritable, and
   "don't look at me," snap days.
Getting a free pass out of gym class, no swim what a win!

What once was that uncomfortable bulky
   thick pad between my legs
Now has a more comfortable solution.

Popping aspirin and Tylenol with ease, look
   now here comes Midol PMS to please.

Making days and nights feel better, without
    the terrible cramps to hinder.

Pap smears, what are these? Have no fear the gynecologist
    is here, she will answer all your female questions!

This purpose to hold and grow a tiny human
    is gone from my loins forever

As the years go by, our body system starts to
    wither to months, years, then no more
I have entered menopause with no turning back

Hold on, don't make me laugh, cough, or
    sneeze, for I shall have to pee

Hot flashes galore.
My body is changing once more.
Weight gain is such a pain.

Welcome to what is called womanhood, I'm
    sure you have your own story to tell
But this is mine in a nutshell.

Quintessential Courage

Cindy Urbanski

I BADLY WANT TO BE AUTHENTIC and courageous.

In yoga training in 2020, I was asked to
    create a code of sorts to live by.

It was supposed to encompass all we were
and more importantly
for those of us remembering that it's a practice not a perfect,
all we *wanted* to be.

Mine is

I am fearlessly accepting, wildly authentic,
    persistently truthful, relentlessly kind.

In truth,
I have been practicing inauthenticity for decades.

In front of people I call friends, I have it all together.

"Yeah, I have a lot on my plate and life isn't perfect, but I'm okay."

In my therapist's office, I am "perfectly fine."

"Sure, there's a ton going on, but I'm using my tools, and I'm
    okay. Thank you for
    listening."

Y'all,

Let me tell you,
I am not at all fine.

In fact, I'm a hot mess.

I am angry and bitter about plain old reality.
And in that anger and bitterness,
I am making my reality worse.

I talk a good game about the practice of radical acceptance.

And yet ...

I am not accepting of the reality that there is pain in
    life that has to be lived through and dealt with.

I am not accepting that people we love get sick and die, and
    it's just plain unfair, and that *hurts*... for a *long* time.

I am not accepting that truly amazing people can do
    unexplainable harm to themselves and leave those they love in
    torment. I am not accepting that grief comes in tsunami waves.

And if we want to get down to the real stuff (which it seems
    I am doing, and if you are still reading, then we are in
    this together), I am bitter about my own limitations.

You know,
My imperfections.

My inability to fire on all cylinders at all times.
My need for sleep.
Illness
Injury

Reality.

I do not practice the courage it takes to be
    vulnerable and authentic and accepting;

I have my reasons. I like to call them Gremlins

Society.
Generational trauma.
Plain old trauma.

Here's what I've learned this week.

Those are only gremlins if I allow them to be.

You see,
I'm driving the bus, and *I* get to say which gremlins
    need to sit in the back or just get on off.

I get to choose when I practice the courage to
    show up as vulnerable and authentic.
And in that act, I can get the support I need to choose
Quintessential Courage
And radical acceptance.

Restoration

Kristin Bowen

A SECRET SO DARK THAT I kept it from myself for over 30 years.

There, I said it.

Rape.

"He raped me."

The words barely snuck out of my mouth when I first spoke them out loud. It had taken an entire session, years of hour-long sessions, peeling back the onion with my counselor of 20 years before I could even utter the full sentence. I spent most of one session referring to "it" or the "thing" he did. She could assume what I was talking about given her background and experience but needed me to say the words to be sure. She wasn't in the business of guessing. She had given multiple options to free myself from this secret and even permission to wait until another session to disclose this dark information; however, being vague was no longer one of those options. After silently convincing myself that it would be powerful and bold to put actual words and a description to this thing that he did, I decided to try and say it out loud. My voice was absent, almost like the words escaped my body, or perhaps they were stuck in the pit of my stomach, clinging to the bottomless pit, unwilling to come to the surface. First, I closed my eyes and visualized the word, the awful, terrifying, scary word. I could say the sounds of each letter in my head, but there was absolutely, positively, no way those words wanted to see the light of day. R—A—P—E.

I hadn't even said the word out loud yet, and my counselor's face was filled with sadness and compassion. She already knew what I was going to say had happened. She had probably known for years the trauma I held within my soul. She handed me a piece of paper and a pen. "Write it," she said with empathy and a strong conviction that was going to push me through this moment of bravery. I didn't feel very brave. I felt like a small child, afraid of my own shadow, hiding in the closet of my past. I glanced at the clock by her end table. In my head, I began calculating how much time was left in this session and deciding if I needed to hurry up and get this over with or prolong the process and prevent having to say the words out loud. Letter by letter, I doodled shapes and curves on the yellow lined, sticky paper. The anger began to bubble up inside of me, then I scratched and scribbled the paper ferociously to make it all go away, crossing out the random letters I had already written on the paper, attempting to remove the memory from my brain. In that moment, it felt like I was erasing the pain, the sadness, and, most importantly, the thought of the word that had so much meaning in just four little letters. It was at that moment I decided to write a word with the same meaning and a much different impact, "sex". That felt acceptable as though nobody would question the story behind it, or more importantly, question me. I could live with that. I took a moment to build up a little more courage and write some more, "He ra _ _ _ me."

It reminded me of that scene with Jim Carrey in the movie *Liar Liar* when he is holding a blue pen in his hand and trying to say that its color is red. He is fighting with himself both internally and physically, throwing his body around the room, struggling with the pen as the word "red" won't move past his lips. I, too, was stuck at the "r" sound. "He r, r, r, r _ _ _ _ me." My hand could barely write the damn letter, let alone mumble the sound. It seemed as if writing it would make the moment more true and raw. I was naked in this room, yet fully clothed. This was all too terrifying. I just wanted it to stop.

If I'm being completely honest, I still had doubts it even happened myself. The dialogue in my head continued to berate and belittle my entire experience.

"Where did this memory come from? Why did I have it hidden and locked away for so long? What if I was wrong about everything and it was just some crazy vision that I made up? Am I a liar? Couldn't we just go back in time and pretend none of this ever happened? I miss those days of ignorance. I didn't want to be damaged, as they say. Who the hell are they anyway? I could just keep pretending that none of this was true. Couldn't I heal myself and overcome this incident without actually reliving or confirming the things that had been done to me? Hell, I could barely believe the words myself. How was anybody else going to believe me? Did it really happen, or did I imagine it? Forget it, I'm probably just making it all up. My memory is trash anyway."

I could barely remember what I ate for dinner last night, let alone something that supposedly happened 30 years ago. Then, my heart kicked in; my intuition started to speak up and remind me who I am at the core. I'm NOT a liar. This memory is vivid and clear. When I close my eyes, I can feel the scruff of his beard, the heat of his breath and the heaviness of his body plopped on top of me. There are no questions whether it's valid or true. This memory is not convenient. It will not help me advance in any way, shape, or form. It tends to return at times when I'm trying to avoid thinking about anything at all. Its favorite time to make an appearance is when my husband and I are being intimate. These are the soft moments, the quiet times when he is pursuing me so gently and lovingly. As he leans over to gently caress my neck, the evening return of stubble on his face gently rubs against my skin. It sends literal shivers down my body, and not the kind of shivers that make you tingle or your heart skip a beat. It is this exact instance that I feel my body shift and lock up immediately. My jaw becomes tense as I purse my lips together in protest, and my eyes squeeze themselves closed even tighter, as if to halt the memory from entering my brain. "No, no, no, no, no not again," I scream inside my head as I try to burst out of my body and stop my past from ruining this moment yet again.

I paused and took a deep breath as I looked at the carpet on the floor in her office. I counted to three in my head and quite literally dove into the healing process. "Fuck it," I mumbled under my breath and began scribbling on the scrap of paper over and over and over again....

He rap

He rap me

raped

He raped me.

He raped ME.

HE RAPED ME!!!!!

My arm felt limp, and my body wanted to drop to the floor. I felt as though I could burst out of my skin and explode. The energy had been sucked out of me. I almost screamed it, those words on the paper, out loud, at the top of my lungs, "HE RAPED ME!!!!" but I caught myself before making a scene. My brain already knew if I did that, I probably wouldn't recover. I would have been a sloppy puddle on the floor unable to peel myself off the carpet. Writing those words with such force, smashing the ball of the pen to the paper, was liberating. That pit that was stuck in my throat slowly started to dissolve. Then I took a huge sigh of relief. I could breathe again, deep down into my belly. I hadn't been able to take a deep breath like that in a long time. It was done. It was in the world now. It was permanent, and the scar I had kept inside was now visible to the world. I had the stark realization that this was only the beginning of my healing journey. The process was nowhere near over. I snuck a look at the clock again and noticed the minute hand was just several notches from reaching the 12. I could tell time was running out for this session, and I didn't know if I was relieved that I had come this far or anxious about the work that was coming up next.

My counselor's words came out slowly with caution, "How would you feel about saying those words out loud, the ones you wrote on the paper?" Fuck, was she serious? I was annoyed and questioned what the hell I was still doing here. I had a passing thought of just getting up and leaving the office. After a short pause, I composed myself, sat up taller in my seat, and began to think more logically. I knew I had to at least try and give a voice to these powerful yet deadly words. I didn't come this far to stay in the hole and hide. I wasn't willing to keep this a secret anymore. I could have easily ended the session and walked out with my head held high. She certainly didn't expect me to do any more work that day.

She could see the exhaustion on my face. I think she would have been proud of me just for getting the words out on paper, but it wasn't enough for me. I had spent years working on my healing, and this was just the breakthrough I needed. I could feel it in my bones. My body was vibrating to let this pain out, and silence was no longer a response I could consider. Who was I protecting anyway? The only person who ever needed protection was me. This was my chance to save myself. This single moment in time started the process of me taking back my power. I'm still shocked it only took one attempt. I whispered the words out loud this time, so soft that they didn't convey their full meaning.

"He raped me."

There was no major release, no flooding of tears or sobbing. Heck, not even a sigh of relief this time. I felt numb, again. I knew this feeling all too well. In fact, this particular feeling was much more comfortable than those other big emotions of the roller coaster I was riding moments before. Then it started to hit me. My head felt a bit woozy, and the room was starting to spin ever so slightly. Everything was in slow motion and speeding up at the same time. I felt sure that I was going to pass out, but of course

I didn't say a word. I paused for a moment to check in with myself and realized my mouth wasn't salivating. This was good news. I could control what happened next. I was the owner of my body now. I could make this stop all on my own. There came an "a-ha" moment where things started to make sense. I began to realize the purpose behind this hidden information that I had kept from myself for all of these years.

This must have been my brain's way of protecting my heart for all of these years. My body had known what happened, every angry thrust and heavy pant that had taken away my innocence. My brain was responsible for shutting this memory down, not because it was untrue, but because the truth was so damaging that it may have killed me. It was only my body, my inner soul, that could sense and recognize these moments from time to time. Maybe it was my inherent ability to sense or notice fear within myself. My gut was a guide that I had dismissed for way too long, and it was sick of being ignored. Little moments in time like my husband's scruffy beard against my neck, the way a stranger may stare in my direction a little too long, or when a seemingly kind yet suspicious man offers help, my body would remember those moments from my past and tense up in preparation to protect me. I didn't need the protection anymore. The truth was clear. I was safe, finally.

This secret, this memory and all of its dirty details, had been tucked away in the depths of my mind for so long, hidden in a place where I wouldn't be able to find them no matter how hard I searched, until now.

I glanced at the clock again, watching each minute pass by. I knew time was up for our session. I had to get into my car and drive home. I had kept it together and avoided falling completely apart. The numbness I experienced now helped me feel unphased by the whole situation so that I could stay safe yet again. I tucked the paper, the one with the scribbles and terrifying truths, into my purse, folding it neatly to be sure it hid the words on the paper. I folded it several times so that it wouldn't unknowingly reveal my secret. It felt safe to put it away, still close by yet nobody else could see it. I wasn't ready to let it go. Something this big, this powerful, didn't deserve to go into the trash. I wanted, I needed, to carry it with me. It was part of me, still my little secret, my little piece of liberation.

Sexual abuse. That's another safe way of saying "rape." They say sexual abuse is usually committed by people who are closest to you, not the random stranger at the park or super market. We were given all these stories of monsters who looked like strangers in the world, but nobody told us the real monsters were the ones that could live in our homes. There are plenty of excuses and stories behind why people did this, or the trauma the perpetrator faced when they were younger. It was all bullshit. So what was the reason behind my story?

My mom was a teenager when she had me. She and my dad quickly realized they were not meant to be together forever when I was about 2 years old. Shortly after they split up, my mom thought she had met the man of her dreams. Little did she know, he would become one of our worst nightmares.

I was only 5, still innocent and naive. It was around this same time, that for the first time ever, I had learned to tie my shoes. I was so proud of myself. Most kids would have run downstairs to share the news, but I had nobody to share this excitement with at the time. The walls were bare, and the room was fairly empty. When the sun came through the window, you could see the reflection of the dust floating in the air. There was no rug or toys to play with and definitely no pictures on the wall. It was my own mini prison even though I wasn't locked in and I hadn't committed a crime. I was sitting on my wooden bed testing out the two bunny ear method when it finally clicked! Two loops, cross, swoosh, and pull. I had made a knot. My first big win, and the moment has stuck with me forever. I had remembered this day with pride for the last 30 years. Little did I know, this room meant more to me than learning how to tie my shoes.

It was on this same bed, later that night, that he raped me. I remember it so clearly now even though I had simply left my body while it was all happening. While he was raping me, I didn't tell him to stop. I certainly didn't put up a fight or struggle. There was no crying. I didn't even make a sound. "Be quiet so you don't disturb anyone," is what I told myself. I don't even remember a single tear after he was done with me and I was alone in my bed. I had completely disconnected and floated away to a safer place in my mind. Sure, my physical body was still there, suffering all of the abuse as my eyes witnessed the torture he was committing to my flesh and bones, but my mind was far far away. In my gut, I had always known this was the reason why I had no memories of my past or recollection of my childhood. Your body keeps tabs of these things. It calculates the damage and tallies up the score. Perhaps it doesn't ever let you truly forget.

Whether I liked it or not, this secret of mine had played out in every facet of my life. It was confusing, yet I understood now why these memories were locked up in a special file, safely hidden in the depths of my brain. My young mind would not have been able to process all of the competing thoughts and beliefs. Was this brutal act that was done to me at such a young age an act of acceptance and love or, in fact, rejection and punishment? For this exact reason, I spent my younger years in conflict, fearful of drawing attention to myself while also wanting to be liked and adored. I learned how to be an overachiever in school while staying humble and quiet. Perfectionism ran rampant throughout every phase of my younger years and into adulthood. I wanted to do everything perfectly and avoid feeling the disappointment of others. I quietly strove to win in all areas of life to ensure I received the love and affection that I deserved, but not too much; I didn't want to be seen or take up too much space.

Naturally, it played a part in each of my sexual relationships. I went through phases of trying to win men over with sex and using my body as a powerful tool to convince others of my worthiness.

Sex was merely an act to please my partner, certainly not for my pleasure. I could quickly and easily zone out or leave my body to protect myself from the experience. I dressed modestly with only a hint of sexy. I didn't want to make the boys turn their heads or feel like they had permission to touch me without consent and also wanted them to chase and desire me all at the same time.

For years, I only had this nagging feeling that deep down in my gut something wasn't right. Something had happened to me on that gorgeous, sunny day in my bedroom with the dusty floors and lonely dresser. Nobody ever told me to keep it a secret, at least I don't think they did. I just knew. This was something never to be spoken of out loud. I knew this so inherently that I didn't even remember what happened until over 30 years later. Although I had always sensed something happened in my past, how could I accuse someone when I have no memory? How dare I trust my instinct? How dare I blame someone else for my problems? How could I heal?

I was starting to remember every detail. My body knew. My bones knew. My heart knew I was on a mission. I needed to find out more. I needed to be sure. As I started to remember, my life began to unravel. I struggled to have sex with my husband. I was constantly triggered into paralysis as his touch would make my skin crawl. I felt used like all he wanted was sex. None of it was true, but that's what my past had always proven, and I couldn't shake the feeling out of my body. I was a tool, a mechanism for other people's pleasure, never taking into account my own feelings, needs, or desires. The details started coming back to me, first in flashbacks, then as short scenes from a movie. I could visualize it. I could see my room. I saw him on top of me and myself lying down on the bed. It was as if I was viewing the whole thing from the eyes of a third party. It was rough and harsh and fast. There were no words.

The part of my life where I begin to remember is when I was safe.

When I finally met my husband, I was sick of playing the games and tired of letting others use my body. He was my rest, my home, my safe place. I was safe, inside and out. It took years before I could share this secret with him, and really there were so many more secrets of sexual assault just like this that had happened over my lifetime. I had written them off as how things were. I already knew that most women had many of the same experiences. It would take me years to disclose them all, and this was just the beginning. Hell, I didn't even know what this BIG secret was for the first half of our relationship. It was just the tip of the iceberg, the catalyst, the foundation that set all the others in motion to come flooding back to my present memory. The intimate moments we shared together were so powerful, yet they could be ripped away from us just as easily when I felt the stubble on his face rub my neck the wrong way. How dare these memories have this much power! The flashbacks became more regular as I started the healing process, and he was afraid to even touch me.

I went on an intense healing journey after years of therapy didn't seem to do the trick. I began practicing yoga, attended meditation retreats, researched plant medicines, and participated in several ayahuasca healing ceremonies. As I think back and recall all of my memories, I'm not sure if it ever happened again, but I know for sure now that it happened, and I can't keep this secret any longer.

My body was used as a tool to please others almost my entire life, not just for sex, but to be pretty and say kind things. I thought I was put in this world to make everyone else happy and comfortable. If you're a woman reading this, perhaps your body has been used in this way too or you hold these same beliefs. I had learned early on not to speak about this topic. Hell, I think I even believed it was normal or "just the way things were meant to be." The truth is, we don't have to be quiet anymore to please others. This is your chance to be loud and bold and take up as much space in this world as possible. You deserve the happiness that is on the other side of the healing you must go through. It's safe over here on the other side. You deserve to heal.

R

Suicidal Tendencies

Kristin Bowen

Trigger Warning: This piece speaks to issues of suicidal ideation.

NOBODY, AND I MEAN NOBODY, WANTS to talk about it: depression. The ones who suffer want to avoid it. Those that comfort the ones who are depressed don't know what to say. It's confusing and dark and gloomy. What is there to even talk about? Who are these people that are depressed? What do they look like? Well, we look like everyone else. We hang out with our friends and laugh at funny jokes. We go to happy hour after work and wear makeup and high heels. We even make dinner and have a clean house. You wouldn't even know we are depressed half the time you see us. That may be the hardest part, besides the fact that most times we don't even know why we are sad.

The thing about depression is that it comes at you out of nowhere. It feels like jumping into the hole of a bottomless pit and sitting there without any glimmer of light. We almost never know what we need to get out of this dark place. Sometimes it's just a helping hand or a few words of encouragement and we can crawl out on our own. Other times we need someone to come sit next to us in the hole, just long enough for us to remember we aren't alone. And when it's really dark, we need someone to hoist us up on their back so we can crawl our way back to the opening of the hole, dirt under our fingernails, scrambling to the top, and start to see the light of day that we have been avoiding.

I venture to say that most people who experience this emotion didn't get there from a major trauma, like the death of a parent or another horrible event that would take just about anyone's breath away. For many, this darkness has become part of them like that little brown birthmark that has been on their wrist since the day they came into this world. One day they wake up and bam, like a stack of bricks, they feel the weight of the world on their back and everything feels hopeless. It's unexplainable and confusing, even to the person who is experiencing it. One second they're smiling and laughing with their partner, and the next day they are wandering around the house aimlessly, lying in bed with nowhere near enough energy to put on socks or even reheat a meal. Getting up to take a shower feels like a million steps too far, and calling a friend or answering a text is out of the question. There seems to be no end in sight and only one solution to end the pain, the numbness and the defeat. Why stay on this earth to suffer, to endure this pain without any relief?

I remember the first time I thought I was going to end it all. I was 10 years old, yes 10, living with my mom and her obnoxious boyfriend who loved to pretend we were one big happy family and he was the dad I "always needed." I had started rebelling by sneaking out of the house while I was ground to play with the boys in the neighborhood. We began to explore the excitement of fire, splashing in the creek, and smashing bugs. At the same time, I had started talking back to my mom regularly, getting more brave with each instance. My dad lived less than an hour away, but I only saw him a couple days per month, and that's if he didn't cancel or come extremely late. There were times I used to ride the train alone, into Washington, DC. Back then, there were no cell phones, only quarters and pay phones, if you were lucky. I would sit at Union Station, for what seemed like hours, wondering if he remembered that I was arriving today. How long should I wait before getting a police officer or calling my mom to come pick me up? I don't even know where the idea came from, or if I saw it on TV or overheard someone talking about it, but I had made up my mind that the best way to die was overdosing on painkillers. That seemed like a logical response to pain. There was a grocery store right behind my house. I had managed to get a few dollars, just enough to buy what I needed. I chose the extra strength bottle thinking it would work more quickly and I wouldn't have to swallow as many pills. I hated swallowing pills, but I couldn't imagine the pain and gore of slitting my wrists, or hell, finding a gun and blowing out my brains. I did consider jumping in front of a fast moving car or train before but worried that if I tripped or stumbled, then I would be left broken and bruised or disfigured but definitely not dead. I also had a bleeding heart for others and considered the pain of the person that would have caused the damage to my hypothetical, disfigured body.

On that day it happened, the weather was beautiful. The sun was out, birds chirping outside, a smile on my face. I was actually happy, relieved I finally had a plan, a way to end these feelings of despair. I was a latchkey kid, letting myself inside the house after school, so I knew I would be home alone for a couple of hours before my mom got home from work. I purchased my weapon of choice and came back home. The bottle clearly said to call poison control if you accidentally ingested too many. Well, this was no accident. After removing the safety cap, I poured more than enough to take away a headache into my hand, counting out 20 red and blue pills for good measure. I planned out my demise, deciding I could quickly gulp and swallow five at a time. My brain had convinced me that I would pass out and peacefully pass away. Looking back, I had no thoughts about my family and friends or what they would think or feel. This wasn't about them. This was about the deep, dark sadness that lived within me at the time. If I had to guess, I assumed they would be content, knowing that I no longer had to suffer the woes of this miserable life, happy for me that I found a solution to all my problems.

As I started swallowing small handfuls of these deadly pills, the fear began to kick in, but I was already too deep. I must have had a moment where I realized the permanence of my decision. My hand was empty, heart racing, and my mind started to race in different directions. I called my friend and told her what I had done, pleading with her to fix it. What should I do? How do I make this stop? I want it to end, but not my life, just the pain. I was panicking, shaking, scared to death. She was even more terrified and sprung into action. She asked me for the number on the bottle and told me to wait by the phone until she called me back. She must have called poison control and they told her to call 911. Several long minutes later, I heard the sirens outside my window. Embarrassment washed over my face as I realized I was going to have to own up to my actions and tell people what I did. That whole period of time is a blur. A group of six first responders marched into my house asking me questions about what I took, where was the bottle, and strapping a blood pressure cuff around my arm. I was on the second floor, and protocol said they had to strap me to the stretcher and take me down the front stairs of my condominium. My head was spinning. They carefully took me to the back of the ambulance. What I remember most is when I saw the undeniable look of horror on my grandmother's face as she pulled up to my house at the same time they were loading me into the back of the ambulance. At this moment, they began taking the necessary steps to save my life and save me from myself. They made me drink an entire cup of the most disgusting, thick, sticky, sweet, black, liquid charcoal out of a Styrofoam cup. As I made it to the hospital, they shoved a massive tube, thicker than the width of a toothbrush, down my throat so that they could pump my stomach, removing all of the toxins and drugs, yet still not taking away the intense pain and feelings of guilt, shame, and sadness. All of this turmoil, and it still wouldn't be the last time I would attempt to end my life.

I attended counseling, spent hours talking about why oh why would I do something so drastic to solve problems that had other solutions. I wanted the attention but not this kind of attention. I didn't need the spotlight. I didn't want everyone looking at me like I was broken or walking around on eggshells. I just wanted it to end. Throughout middle school, I attempted this scenario a few more times without resolve. Hell, I thought, "I wasn't even good at killing myself." By the time I entered high school, I decided to turn to drugs instead. If I couldn't kill myself, then I would numb the pain with other substances and stop the pain receptors from feeling anything at all. This method worked for a long time, and I went back to hiding, being unnoticed. When I wasn't high or strung out, I sat in that dark hole I had built inside of myself and bled out internally so that nobody could see the pain. I don't even think anybody noticed for a while. Life was simply a game that I was losing, and I had zero strategies to manage the ups and downs.

As my first year of college was ending, there was a moment of hope. I just had to make it to summer time. I was coming home to a familiar place, or so I thought. I had no idea that plans had changed. I had been living with my dad before heading off to school, and now he had moved to a new apartment building. Okay, no big deal. This still seemed exciting, and I couldn't wait to get back to the place that I felt was home. As I welcomed myself into the new space, I was greeted by black trash bags, filled with my belongings, sitting in the middle of the living room. I was taken aback but was still unphased by these changes. He had moved my things in an unconventional way, but I could unpack and make a safe space here. No, that was not the plan.

I had no bedroom to myself, only space on the empty living room floor. It was during that next week that suicidal ideation began to take hold of my brain, and I began imagining how I would end it all, again, for the fifth time. It wasn't his fault. My dad had no idea what was going on in my brain. Just like it wasn't my mom's fault before when she was clueless to the real pain that I was feeling. I see that now. I wish I could have explained it to them back then. It was me. It was my lack of self-worth. It was my desire to be loved when I was unsure of how to love myself. It was all of these moments strung together, leading up to a perfect storm of guilt, anger, defeat, and shame.

We were now on the 14th floor of an apartment building. Here I stood on the balcony, weighing the pros and cons of climbing to the edge and leaping towards the ground. My logical brain kept getting in the way. What if I stood up there and slipped as I changed my mind? What if I regretted this decision the moment I jumped off the rail? It seemed a bit dramatic. Thank God I didn't have the guts to go through with it. I could only imagine the blood and guts on the ground as people walked by my lifeless body. I still considered other people's feelings more valuable than my own. Then I became desperate, frantic, looking for another way out and a way to end this nauseating pain. I found the household products with poison warnings on the bottle. I read the label on the back of the antifreeze coolant. The writing was small, but the poison symbol with a skull and crossbones was clear. The liquid was bright blue and looked like a glass of sugary Kool-Aid. I still can't tell you why I even poured it into a glass. The smell was enough to make me pass out, and I could barely get a drop across my lips. I opened my mouth wide and took a big gulp, then instantly spit it across the floor. I couldn't even force my throat to swallow this vile liquid. That critic that lived in my brain started to speak up again. "You couldn't even kill yourself. You're such a loser."

At that moment, I gave up in the best way possible. I was defeated yet again, though perhaps this time it was divine intervention. As the weeks passed, I thought about other quick and easy ways to die. I fantasized about running my car into a tree or into the oncoming traffic of a busy street. I may be able to find a gun and shoot myself in the head. There was no way I was going to stab myself or slit my wrists. I could look for a fast-paced train nearby. Thankfully, I cared more about the other people who would be affected by the trauma and the accident, so I didn't go through with any of it.

Life continued to carry on as usual with the typical peaks and valleys. I struggled to survive them, putting one foot in front of the other. Soon after college, I became a single mother, recovering from a drug addiction. I had moved back home with my parents to create a little stability and start building a life for my daughter. After the birth of my daughter, life felt complete. She was such a happy little baby, and while the nights were tough and motherhood was certainly hard, I finally found a reason to live. That was, until, the voice inside my head, the one that makes me doubt everything, caused me to believe that everyone in my life would be better off without me.

I was home alone with my sweet, precious baby. I knew somebody else would be home in just a few hours, so she would be safe if I wasn't there any longer. She was napping upstairs when I searched for painkillers, good ole faithful. I knew what this was like and thought to myself that I could get ahead of the fear of what would happen next and actually go through with it. This time I decided to grab a handful and chug them with vodka instead of water to make sure I got the job done. The scene replayed just like when I was in elementary school, except the stakes were higher, and the pain was arguably deeper. I don't know what happened next. I imagine I may have lay down or passed out and someone came home and saw what I did. An ambulance was called, and the hospital was responsible once again for flushing my stomach with a charcoal paste to pump the poison from my belly. After pumping my stomach this time, they couldn't just let me go home with my parents. I wasn't a kid anymore. I was, in fact, a parent, who had a child of their own, a person I was responsible for keeping alive, and I attempted to end my own life.

The hospital requested that I transfer to an in-patient facility where I could talk to more counselors about more feelings and try to come up with better solutions for my problems. I didn't want to go, but it seemed like the right thing to do, and I thought it may be the only way to recover. Plus, I'm not sure I had any other options. They may have taken away the one thing in my life that provided hope and a reason to live again. So I worked the program, attended the group and individual sessions, journaled all day, and after a week, they sent me home with a folder and a phone number to call the next time I had these thoughts. The problem was, after all of that intense therapy, I still didn't learn to love myself, trust myself, or ask for help. How does one learn to love oneself in a week after years of feeling they weren't good enough?

Life continued on again, and I battled the ups and downs with grace by distracting myself from the pain. I kept busy and had lots of plans on my schedule. There was no time for loneliness or big feelings. I had even survived the possibility of postpartum after the birth of my next two children. It was deceiving, as if I had "gotten over it." I thought it must have been a phase and I was "all better" now. Little did I know that when my youngest, my fourth child was born, it would all come rushing back.

It made no sense. Nobody would have ever guessed I would suffer from depression again. My husband and I were rock solid. We had an amazing relationship. We worked like a team and were happy. We created an environment that had all of the characteristics you would want to prevent depression. If there was a rubric to measure, you could say I was truly set up for success—good job, stable home, solid income. My husband and I were happily married and truly excited to bring a new life into this world. Our sweet baby girl was born into the most loving, beautiful home, and we couldn't have been happier. We even spent the first few weeks waking up together to feed her. My husband would use this as our time to connect with each other at 3 a.m. as I breastfed our new baby, and we laughed together at ridiculous infomercials on the television or watched basketball replays. We were tired, but we had each other. Here I was with all of the love and support that anyone could ask for, and then it hit me. This time it hit me hard and fast, smacked me in the face and broke me down to nothing.

I sobbed for days on the couch with no apparent reason, no thing that I could point to and say, "This is making me sad." I refused to shower at times and pleaded with my husband to stay home from work and fix me. I couldn't even imagine returning back to work, and watching my favorite shows seemed like a waste of time. I did not want to do anything. Of course there were moments of joy and happiness. I loved watching my little girl giggle and learn new things. Family dinners were chaotic, but I loved the noise of our family spending time together.

As time went on, I also did all of the things I had been taught over the years to do during these tough moments. I called my friends, forced myself to get out into the sunshine, and played music to lift my spirits, even when I didn't want to do it. I would journal my feelings, encourage myself to eat nutritious foods while also indulging in ice cream and potato chips to comfort the big emotions. I showered and washed my face, put on my favorite clothes for no good reason, and ran errands to be around people and get out of the house. The difference this time was that while I felt all the feelings, and even had the thoughts of ending it all, I didn't act on them. I proved to myself that while these moments may still happen, I am strong enough to get through them.

I'm not broken. I never was. And I don't need to be fixed. The only secret to the healing process is that we each hold our own key. We are the only ones who can save ourselves. Nobody, not even my mom or dad, my best friend, or my life partner could save me. I had to do my own healing. The things that worked for me may not work for anybody else, and that is what is so frustrating. There is no map or checklist that you can follow to cure depression. I still get depressed. Sometimes I can feel it start to bubble up inside of me. It begins to creep around like a thief and try to make its way to the surface so it can steal my joy. What I have learned in the healing process is how to notice these shadows in their early stages. It gives me time to start the process of getting back to myself, doing the things that bring me happiness, slowing down life a bit to take care of me, and focusing on what I need and not everybody else, just for a little while. Now I have figured out how to keep it from taking over. I'm not naive to the fact that I may not catch it early enough in the future and it could take over for a while, but that is okay because I know now that I'm not better off dead. I have learned how to ride the ebb and flow, realizing that for every valley, there is a peak on the other side. Now, I trust these moments will pass and hold tight. The feelings are my guide to notice what is going on within me. I actually allow myself to feel the tough emotions, and the faster I do that, the quicker it will pass. Healing depression will always be an inside job.

Tags

Taylor Edwards

IN THE BEST OF WHAT I do,
My soul has no tag
That determines
>Small,
>Medium,
>or *Large*
My soul itself
Is endless
My soul takes up space and shifts its being
 from every cardinal direction:
>*VAST*

The other day,
I met a lady in the bathroom.
I slink out of the stall and will her space that she already took up
In front of the bathroom sink.
As she dries her large hands across scratchy
cardboard paper towels,
I suck in and squeeze past her, parceling out
half the breath I hold in to say:
Excuse me.

Large woman in the bathroom: *This bathroom is small.*
  Because that's what they say women should be.
Me, in response: *I know.*
Large woman in the bathroom: *I guess they don't know us.*
Me, in response: *I know.*

FUCK THE PATRIARCHY
IS ETCHED IN EVERY FABRIC OF MY LIFE
WHY, THEN, AM I ANGRY
WHEN A WOMAN LOOKS TO ME AS HER REFLECTION,
ADMONISHING THE POWER THAT DICTATES
WHAT BODIES SHOULD BE?
THE BODIES THAT **WE DON'T HAVE**?

"Women should be small"
Is the biggest lie
That I've let rot in my stomach…
The one thing I've yet to
purge
out of me.

Thank you, lady in the bathroom, for your kindness.

T

Untethering

Shana Hartman

THERE IS A DENT IN MY ring finger that reminds me
of my path to untethering

Reminds me of what was and fuels what will be

A groove seemingly permanent, etched in
    the tissues and layers that were us

The us that has been lost.

The us that has been grieved and surrendered to.

The us that is no longer an us, but distinctly you and distinctly me.

Distinguishing me is a practice of untethering,

Yet, no one told me how to do this.

I knew plenty of others who had a dent just like
    mine, but they were like ghost dents…
We all knew they were there, but no one dared discuss them much.

My dent is not a ghost in the shadows. I won't let it be.

I bravely bring the mark into the light because
each time I look down, the dent is there, reminding me

Reminding me of the ill-formed words spoken.

Reminding me of the pain and sorrow.

Reminding me of the choice I had to make to live.

Reminding me of just how much more untethering is needed.

And, I don't ever want to forget or hide this
   from my current or future self.

As the untethering continues
from the mistrust,
the lack of safety,
the lies,
and the abuse, my dent fades,
slowly and intentionally

I instead tether and anchor myself
To the Divine

Divine trust.

Divine safety.

Divine truth and freedom.

As I tether to this new way of being, my skin slowly smooths,
my dent less noticeable,

alongside a heart healing
(because we never are quite healed, right?)

I tether to that smoother skin and that healing heart

I tether to me.

Voice

Karen Taylor

As I WAS WORKING ON THIS piece one day, I saw the news where
Tina Turner died, and it deeply affected me. Her words and life
story sustained me through some very tough times because she was
a beacon of strength and power due to the adversity she overcame
in her life. By no means do I equate myself to her or her heroic acts
of rising out of the devastation that had become her life, but I do
feel that we shared some of the same feelings because I had to pull
myself out of a traumatic situation as well. To be writing about
voice, especially women's voices, and including something about
Tina Turner seems apropos. So, here I go, with Tina fueling me.

* * *

At one transitional point in my life, I was preparing myself
mentally to leave my marriage. I would get on an exercise bike
and listen to Tina Turner's songs, particularly "I Don't Wanna
Fight No More." I knew I was in a marriage that was never going
to work, and after months of stagnation and getting nowhere, I
read Tina Turner's book. I thought, if she can go through what
she went through and be successful, surely I can too. So to prepare
myself for the adversity I knew was inevitable, I began a diet and
exercise program because exercise usually made me feel better
about myself, and I used Tina Turner's music to work out my

V

conflicted feelings and prepare myself for the trouble I knew I was going to face.

Tina Turner's biography, *I, Tina*, which was adapted into the film, *What's Love Got to Do With It*, includes a detailed depiction of the type of lives some women endure. Because of her strong, powerful, unique singing voice, Ike Turner exploited her talent, while also physically abusing her in their relationship. He viewed her as his ticket to money and success, and she was not treated equally. Her strength and power that arose out of those hard times carried her into success that eclipsed what she and Ike had experienced together. When they were Ike and Tina Turner, she had to sing according to his wishes and choices, and her personal voice was silenced while he rode the rising tide of recording and performing success created by her powerful, beautiful performing voice. She overcame her circumstances and cut through the bullshit, but to do so, she had to begin all over again. This time, her strong singing voice wasn't the only voice that gained acclaim. She became a beacon for women in the dark, voices silenced by their circumstances.

I used Turner's life experiences to sustain me as I went through my painful divorce. The bottom line causation of everything that broke apart was that my husband lost his job as a cop through some weird incidents and poor judgment calls, but I was doing well in my career in the same field. He couldn't handle that, and the financial trouble we had was burying us both. It was an eternal presence in our relationship, like an evil spirit constantly fanning the flames of dissent. I was fortunate enough not to be physically abused repeatedly like Tina Turner, but I did sustain a physical injury during one argument. My husband dislocated my shoulder by grabbing me from behind and twisting my arm behind my back as I held my child in my other arm. It caught me totally by surprise, and although the pain was intense, the shock that he would actually do that to me was worse. I made up my mind at that very moment that I was going to get a divorce.

The shame I felt over this incident was overwhelming, but the benefit of it was that I was better able to understand how battered women feel to some degree. My incident was only one of physical violence, whereas many women live in it for years. Here I was, a police officer, and I couldn't even keep myself from becoming a victim. I struggled with those feelings for a long, long time. After the incident, my husband didn't get that it was the end. It took a while, complete with dealing with a stalking, estranged husband and a lot of other crap I won't go into, but I made the break. I used the strength I found in knowing women who had been battered much more than I had made it through, but I also reached down and grabbed that part of me that had always wanted to be a champion for people victimized by bullies. It had been lying dormant for a little while, but it was rising from its cave like a fire-breathing dragon ready to belch fire and scorch everything in its path. This inner spirit gave me the courage to pursue my dreams and leave behind the things holding me back.

One of the things police officers are taught in training is that domestic violence calls are one of the most dangerous calls they will respond to. I didn't call the police when my injury occurred. The main reason was my shame, and looking back, that was ridiculous, but I knew then and still know that if I had called the police, the incident would have been much worse, and I know that the calls we went on sometimes made those women's situations worse.

One question many people ask is why battered women don't leave their situations. The victims I encountered gave many reasons for this: they were afraid they couldn't make it on their own, they were afraid of being alone, they believed they really loved men who beat them, they couldn't afford daycare for their children, so they couldn't get jobs and depended upon the man's paycheck, and the list goes on. These women were victims of physical, mental, emotional, and verbal abuse and were prisoners of their own lives. They were walking tightropes over raging infernos, just biding time until the flame burned through the rope, sending them down into the depths of a deeper hell than they were already experiencing. See the other crap I didn't want to talk about above.

The feeling of not having a choice was only part of the reason they stayed in their situations. They were also afraid of the obstacles they would face if they did leave. They did have choices, but they were difficult ones to make. They were frozen by this fear and unable to move from what they were experiencing and what they knew to the unknown of what they would have to do to change their situations. Many women did try, and the way the system was set up, after spending a few days at the women's shelter and the program assisting them in starting a new life, the husband/ boyfriend would locate them.

Even when these offenders were arrested, they were out on bail before their victims even got situated at the women's shelter. Eventually, the men would find their wives or girlfriends, and proffer the same excuses: "Baby, I am so sorry I hurt you. I love you. I promise I will never do it again." My ex even gave his tearful apology. He couldn't see that he was wasting his breath. After 7 years, you would think he would've known me better. The one thing I can say about myself with pride is that I learn from my mistakes, and I knew I wouldn't stay around and take a chance on this happening again. But many women would buy into the lies, and after returning to their homes and their husbands or boyfriends, a couple of weeks would pass, and we would be called back to the same houses. Many times, the woman would be beaten worse, but no matter how many times we responded and attempted to help, the pattern continued. I don't believe these women realized they even had a voice because it had been beaten down and suppressed for so long.

The programs for battered women didn't come close to solving all of their problems. The legal step of getting an Order of Protection at that time was better than what preceded it, but it still lacked a great deal of effectiveness. The Order of Protection only kept the men incarcerated for 24 hours, a "cooling off" period. The idea was that the cooling off period would prevent further violence and give the victim a chance to do whatever she needed to do to get herself out of the situation without interference. In many cases, the cooling off never happened. Once out, most of the men would go looking for the women, still very angry.

How do women end up in these kinds of relationships is a question that, if answered, could go a long way in providing a solution to the problem. Most battered women are victims of low self-esteem and the belief that their entire worth is predicated upon their ability to attract a husband or boyfriend. Many of them were raised to believe that this was the only way to make it in the world, that they couldn't make it on their own. Our culture supports this idea by encouraging lower paying jobs for women and no assistance for mothers with children who are trying to work to support their families. We have made some progress, but we need to do a lot more.

Some women who end up in these violent relationships do not feel the power that is in each and every one of us, and predatory males easily spot the women who lack self- confidence. They will begin by exhibiting what appears to be complete and total devotion for their girlfriend, which escalates to the point of obsession, and it is a dangerous trap. Many women unknowingly fall into these traps and are unaware of the danger until it is too late. They are married with children, believing they somehow caused the problem. I am not a psychiatrist or psychologist, but this observation is clinically documented. This feeling that they somehow caused the problem is a seed that is planted by our culture. I saw this occur pretty frequently in my personal life and on the street.

I remember one evening, one of my partners and I were on patrol. It was probably around 10:00 p.m. or so in the summertime, so it was dark. We were checking the area around one of the churches in our zone. The parking lot across the street from the church had a trailer parked there without the tractor. As my partner drove around it, shining the spotlight, he noticed something and stopped. We got out and found a young female, hiding under the trailer. She was around 15 years old or so, and when we asked what she was doing there, she told us she had been at a family cookout when her uncle molested her. She ran out and ended up hiding under the trailer.

We took the young girl home where she lived with her grandmother. I don't think I will ever forget her grandmother's reaction when we informed her of why we brought the young lady home. The grandmother began chastising the child. She said, "I told you not to be going around men and talking to them." I was speechless. Here was the kid who was at a family gathering and her own uncle molested her, and her grandmother was blaming her. I remember thinking to myself that this kid didn't stand a chance out in the world, and this kind of thing just snowballs, resulting in women having distorted views of their worth, ending up living punching bags. These kinds of things are what clears the way for much of the violence women experience in their relationships, the idea that the girl/woman somehow asked to be violated.

The patriarchal machine drives these problematic occurrences. If women were not treated as lesser human beings, this type of abuse would not occur as often. I would say that they might still occur, but with less frequency, and the solution to the problem would be less complicated. Our voices matter, but as long as we have women in subservient roles, whether private, public, or religious, these types of things will continue. We don't have to silence our voices. We don't require a male in our lives to give us value. We are valuable as we are, and our voices matter. If more girls were raised believing that their abilities are enough and that their dreams are achievable, that they are precious gifts to the world before, during, and after any chosen relationship, and if they could be free to speak out when they feel uncomfortable, devalued, or threatened, if they could feel free to use their voices, and our society had systems in place that supported this freedom, our culture could overcome so much of the domestic and other types of violence against women and other oppressed groups. I think Tina and I share this same dream, and I will continue her fight and those of other women with my own words.

V

What. Not Who.

Cindy Urbanski

WHAT!
What?
What happened.

What is the thing that transpired?
What is the misstep …
… the mistake
The Problem?

Now identified, what's next?

What needs addressing?
Rebuilding?
Reconnoitering?
Restitution?

What needs learning.

Not Who, but What

Who says …
Didn't *I* do it?

Wasn't *I* the one who was wrong?
Isn't wrong bad?
Doesn't that make *me* bad?

What do I say,
To my children?
To my husband?
To a friend?
To a client?

I say . . .
"*What* happened?"
"Wrong is where the learning is."
"Learning is THE thing."

My husband has been saying the same to me.
For 30 years.
I didn't hear it,
Believe it,
Choose it.

Generational Trauma is real.
It ends here, with us.

Freedom
Safety
Peace

What.
Not Who.

X'd Out:
Hindsight is 2020

Taylor Edwards

I DON'T KNOW WHAT THE FUCK I'm doing.

Most of the time, within the practice of living.

Definitely, though, when it comes to being a recently out, queer woman, who has just turned 30 …

As a blanket disclaimer to those reading: *I don't know what the fuck I'm doing.*

And, here I am. Here is me. A recently out, queer woman, here to talk to you about how even when I don't know what the fuck I'm doing, the Universe likes to remind me that maybe, actually, *I might have known some things all along.*

In September 2020, I was hyper-focused on dating. Or really, my lack thereof. My dating history up to that point was a 3-year-relationship, a handful of couple-month-flings, multiple sexual rendezvous, and a decade's long fixation on one guy that was everything and nothing that I just described. The energy felt "off" with men, for one. There was an unsettled feeling within myself that hindered connection with other people in general, for two.

The second a situation shifted into something more than platonic, I could automatically feel the air thicken and read into whatever ulterior motives were being presented to me. The entire exchange became stiffened and stale, awkward and performative.

It didn't feel comfortable.

So, during the pandemic, I realized that a lifetime of solitude wasn't necessarily something that I wanted to sign up for, for the rest of my life. A life partner would be needed to combat the ache of loneliness, and I did really, really like the act of orgasm. So, I needed to figure out this comfortability thing … and fast.

"Figuring it out" was something that was constantly at the forefront of my mind. A new obsession to fixate on, I spent time with my journal, pouring words and experiences into its lined pages that I thought might be able to get me to the root of the matter. The underlying cause of it was simple: I knew that there was something *wrong with me*. And if I could just do … *something*, then I would be fixed.

During this same time, I was in a life coaching group program, and, under the guidance of my life coach, I narrowed down two emotions I needed to feel: comfortability and excitement. I wanted to not only feel comfortable, but also excited within a relationship.

Excitement in a relationship looked to me like responsiveness and attunement to another person. Where time would fly by, rather than drag, and the air would expand, rather than exit the room. My heart would swell, but my skin wouldn't become prickly; the charge in the atmosphere would spark, rather than alarms going off to get the fuck out of the situation.

And, I thought, in order to obtain that, I first needed to feel comfortable around men.

After leaving the call that day, I tried to think of practical ways I could feel comfortable around men. The first, most obvious way, would be to start going on more dates. Practically speaking, *practice could help*. And, then . . .

I wrote in my journal that I wanted to stop *pause* masturbating.

That's literally how I wrote it. Stop, X'd out "stop," then, changing my mind, wrote: *pause* masturbating.

September 30th, 2020: The day I, for a moment, decided I should *pause* masturbating.

To understand the gravity of this decision, allow me to admit something to you that isn't for the faint of heart: I love masturbating.

Like, *love* it.

I have a sweatshirt that I delight in wearing that says "hydrate and masturbate" (two causes I'm passionate about). At this point, I've spent more nights lying beside my Satisfyer Pro than I have any other human. My friends even jokingly refer to this love of masturbation as "T-time" because I am not shy about the fact that I firmly believe masturbation is a basic human right. Etch it right alongside life, liberty, and the pursuit of happiness, and I would be the first to sign that constitution.

I love masturbation.

And, September 2020, I was so convinced that something was wrong with me that I was willing to *pause* masturbating because the only logic I could logic out of the situation was that I was just *too* … erm, satiated. And that maybe, just maybe, if I paused fucking myself for a while, I would reach such a state of basic need that men would suddenly become easier to be around.

Seriously.

It *actually* crossed my mind that maybe I needed to stop making myself come *before* it occurred to me that the answer might be to date women.

Funny enough, when I look at the vessel that held these words, it's a journal that depicts *The Birth of Venus* on the cover. At the time, I didn't think about the image, and I really didn't even remember that I had that journal until I sat down to write this. But, have you ever looked at that painting by Botticelli? Venus, the Goddess of Love, rises from her birth out of sea foam and is painted naked on top of a scallop shell, surrounded by other deities. She's beautiful, obviously, and there's a sensuality to the painting that I can't help but linger on. In fact, I've got a copy of it sitting atop a sapphic bookshelf in my living room now. To me, it's a birth of sensuality, a becoming of oneself, one's longing.

To recap: I was denying myself masturbation in an attempt to find some small piece of comfort in a heterosexual relationship. I was writing this in a journal that depicted an image that I now correlate to my queer emblem.

The Universe knew something; I just wasn't picking up the call.

In fact, I was actively hitting "decline" on the call, turning off the phone, and hiding it away… right along with my Satisfyer Pro. Neither things were a buzzin' because I saw my issues with relationships as something that needed *troubleshooting*, fully reliant upon myself for any issues of incompatibility.

And revisiting those earlier goals: how was I supposed to feel comfortable and excited about a relationship in the first place if I was operating from this mindset? While my heart was in the right place, I wasn't giving myself a fair shot at an answer from the get go.

A couple days later, my life coach and I had a virtual one-on-one session, and she asked me, "What does love look like to you?"

I lost it.

I completely lost it.

There was barely a glimpse of something that resembled what love could look like before my body crumbled into tears and I had to take a break—stepping away from the computer—and I couldn't resume the conversation. It was too much, too hard, too scary to go down that… I didn't even understand what I was even going "down" in that moment, but I knew that I had never been asked that question before, and I did not want to explore it, despite thrusting myself into an exploration that begged the very question.

Some time after gathering myself, we stumbled upon a statement, and looking back now, I can't remember who said it, my life coach or me, but as I glance upon the words I wrote back that day in 2020, I can't help but shiver:

You are not a problem to be fixed.

The blindspot that I missed here was that journaling, the meetings, the stop *pause* masturbating, it was all amounting to myself being a problem and the troubleshooting being the ways in which I was hoping to "fix" myself. I am not a problem to be fixed.

I am not a problem, period.

In fact, what if the uncomfortability that my body felt was a signal after all? Not of something that was wrong with me? But of something that was so, so right? That instead of awkward and performative uneasiness, there could be excitement, intimacy, and supercharged sparks in which *I finally felt like myself* around another person—one that just happened to be a woman?

The uncomfortability was there before, as an indicator to show me that the problem wasn't within me, but with what I saw for my life in the compulsive heteronormativity that I dared not to question up until the very moment hindsight crashed into a bright visibility that was impossible to turn away from.

I am a full, sensual being who happens to be attracted to women and has now found that excitement and comfortability that I desired within female partnerships.

Looking back on 2020, there is hindsight.

I still don't know what the fuck I'm doing.

But, I know *who* the fuck I should be doing.

And it's me. And other women.

And, I'm going to enjoy every minute of it.

Yes!

Cindy Urbanski & Mackenzie Urbanski Menon

Note to reader: this piece weaves two voices, mother and daughter, into a sort of tapestry as their thoughts overlap.

When my daughter, Mackenzie, was born, and I named her, I always heard the name with Dr. in front of it in my mind. At zero minutes old, I didn't know what she would be a doctor of, but I knew as I looked into her eyes, that Dr. Anna Mackenzie Urbanski was who she was in her tiny core.

> I've been headstrong for as long as I can remember, and those that were around from before I can remember say that I've been that way since birth. I got it from my grandmother— once that woman made a decision, she was immovable. I grew up looking up to her and my mom, Cindy. Both were strong, independent women with thriving work-life balances and loving husbands. It was exactly what I wanted for myself, and since I have a streak of Mamgu (the Welsh word for grandmother) in me, there was no deterring me from that path.

I got married young. Twenty-one years old. Granted, I was an old soul, and I knew myself and what I wanted. Bret, my husband,

and I listened to all of the advice from the world about how there was no rush… blah, blah, blah. But in the end, we knew we were soulmates, and it made no sense to wait. So we didn't.

Twenty-seven years later I can say we were correct.

I was still pretty young when Mackenzie was born, 27. I had a masters degree, earned after marriage, and a career I loved. And yet, the 80 hours a week required to teach high school the way I wanted to teach it was not conducive to mothering the way I wanted to mother.

I leaned in hard when some older, wiser, professional women in our family started talking about work-family balance. I remember the day my cousins Kathy and Mary Ann said in unison, "Half time is the best of both worlds." Kathy was a pharmaceutical rep with four children, and Mary Ann was a dentist with three children. They had my attention. Part time became my jam, and it was indeed delightful.

Through my early education years, I was often told that I was a "gifted student", and that praise became central to my personality. I excelled in class, and adults adored me—I soaked it up like the tiny absorbent sponge I was, not only because I loved the confidence boost but also because I wanted to be like my mom. Hardworking and whip smart, going back to school to earn her PhD, and so good at her job that she "taught teachers how to teach."

Yes, that was the phrase I used whenever someone asked me what my mom did for work; much to the chagrin of my grade school teachers.

We adopted our son Mason after Mackenzie called a family meeting at 3 years old and insisted on a baby brother, and I stopped teaching high school to care for the two of them. I also started a doctoral program and took a much more flexible job at the local university as Associate Director of the Writing Project, working with teachers on the teaching of writing.

It was *a lot* to juggle. Let's just say we *all* survived the earning of the PhD and leave it at that.

> In high school, I decided that I wanted to be a veterinarian. I took the Biology classes and did the volunteer hours of shadowing that I knew I needed to get into the college, and then eventually the graduate school I wanted. When I got into the University of North Carolina at Chapel Hill, I cried. It was my dream school, and I could see the path in front of me opening up.

Post survival of the PhD, I started talking to Mackenzie about her dreams. From the beginning, I told her to put her focus on what she wanted for herself, her dreams, her goals, and her passions. I can see how this came off as hypocritical to a headstrong 17-year-old. I was basically saying, "Do as I say, not as I've done." I didn't yet know the secret.

Mackenzie wanted to be a veterinarian. Dr. Kenzie, as it would turn out, just as I envisioned in her early hours of entering the world. She dreamed of a rock solid family and marriage on a working ranch with a thriving vet practice and 4-6 children.

Leaning on my own experience and wanting her path to be a little less bumpy, I said,

"You have time!"

"School first!"

"Then marriage and children."

"Establish yourself and *then* find partnership."

> At that time I had a boyfriend, one that would move with me to college and that I would continue to date for many years. He was there while I spent my summers taking extra classes, working at a mobile vet practice, and studying for the GRE. While I loved him, I knew somewhere deep down that he was not the endgame for me.

My mom's words echoed in my ears.

I knew that she and my dad had gotten married young. They had been sure that they were right for each other, and so had decided to pull the hypothetical trigger early for, what I understood as, the sake of convenience. Two apartments cost more money than they were making.

However, her advice to me was always to take it slow, focus on myself and my career and trust that a strong partnership would come in time.

Ever headstrong, I ignored her.

Shocking, I know. To me at 17, her words rang hypocritical. I surely knew more about my own emotions and love than she did.

I spent a lot of energy attempting to mold my life into what I wanted it to be, and in the process, attempted to mold my then boyfriend into something he wasn't.

I'm not proud of that.

I watched Mackenzie bloom in college. She is a natural student. She made amazing friends on the second day. She studied hard. She played hard. On the surface, things were great. But something was missing. My girl is a bonfire, and while to most of the world it looked like she was blazing, I saw her playing small in a relationship with a perfectly wonderful boy. He matched her intellect, her drive, and her big heart, and yet, her bonfire was withering.

Eventually, while waiting for responses to my first round of veterinary school applications, I gave in and broke off the relationship. I finally realized that making him into something I wanted at the expense of who he was would only end up causing resentment from us both. There, on the cusp of the final push to make my professional dreams come true, it was impossible to ignore that I was avoiding a similar push for my personal dreams. I wiped the blinders off my eyes and really looked my heart in the mirror. What I found there was a long hidden secret—one that I suspect was hidden only from me.

Mackenzie was courageous enough to end her comfortable relationship and go after what her heart was telling her it wanted. Rahul entered the picture, and I saw the way she lit up when she talked about him, not to mention the way they both were together. Not only could they not stop touching each other, but I saw my daughter's nose crinkle in a way it hadn't since she crossed into adolescence.

They are fire.

And so, I have done a 180 on all my advice.

The absolute upheaval of my life that followed still rocks me to this day. My dad drove to my university and sat with me in the grass, sharing lunch and quietly listening while I told him how I felt. With his support and blessing, I took a leap of faith and professed my love to the man I had known was meant to be mine since we met 4 years prior.

Both of us had been afraid to do something "wrong" that would cause distress to those around us, and both of us had been afraid of rushing into something that may not turn out to be what we had hoped. But, I was tired of living in fear. My stubborn streak rose, ready to make him understand the depth and ferocity of my feelings; to my surprise, Rahul Menon returned my love without the need for a battle.

What the world thought was a pretty decent bonfire burst into a conflagration of pure and utter joy. There she was! My girl, in all of her amazing glory. She was back. She knew who she was and what she wanted, and she was going for it with every bit of the tenacity she possessed. She was ignoring all the "shoulds" and "supposed to's" and trusting her smart, smart gut and heart

Despite my dad's support and the absolute certainty that I felt in my heart, I was in for months of social turmoil. My friends didn't understand what felt like a sudden change to them, my ex boyfriend was deeply hurt, and I found myself retreating. Despite all my efforts to make this transition the "right" way, I couldn't please anyone. And so, I decided to stop trying and be confident in my love and my strength.

Eight months later, we are engaged to be married next summer, July 13, 2024. To my even greater surprise, we are engaged with the wholehearted support of my family.

Every cautionary bit of advice from my mom has been rescinded.

My usually terrifyingly protective father welcomed Rahul with open arms and considers him a son.

Yes, we will pay for you to see him in NJ, three states away.

Yes, we are ready for you to get engaged if you're ready.

Yes, get married while you're both in graduate school.

"Yes!" Engaged with my blessing after dating for only 8 months. "Yes!" A wedding next summer.
"Yes!" to being married while he pursues a medical degree and she pursues a veterinarian degree.

"Yes, Yes, Yes!" to the Doctors Menon.

Because what I know to be true is that finding your person makes all the other struggles of life and degrees and family-work balance background noise. And these two have found each other. They will make it, come what may.

> My veterinary applications returned as rejections one after the other. A younger me would have been crushed by this blow, but I am bound and determined. I will work for a year and try again. And again if need be.

> My friends have come around, and are happy to join me in planning this wedding and staying in touch across four states. They, too, could see the pure joy that I felt in my choice. I don't know what other surprises there will be in the next few years, but I do know that I will have my partner by my side, and one day we will be The Doctors Menon.

It will be easy AND hard, and it doesn't matter because they will be together, taking on the world! People give us all the side-eye right now. Bret and I have friends who are "checking" to see if we are "okay" with the lightning fast turn of events and are perplexed by our goofy smiles.

It's really not perplexing. Our baby has figured out who she is and is building an amazing life with a perfectly matched mate.

This is the Power of Yes!

Zenith

Shana Hartman

IN THE MOVIE, *LILIES OF THE Field*, Oscar winner Sydney Poitier leads a well-known scene where he teaches the Catholic nuns the gospel song, "Amen." Originally sung and dubbed into the movie by Jester Hairston for Poitier to lip sync, the nuns slowly go along with his conducting, shifting from reluctance to sing anything other than a traditional white, European-centric hymn to eager singers (or lip syncers) and clappers. As the scene unfolds, you can see the uncertainty dissolve into pure freedom and joy.

Writing alongside the authors of this book has been a similar journey—riding alongside one another, letting uncertainty dissolve into pure freedom and joy.

I am always amazed at who says "yes" when Cindy, my co-writing coach, and I cook up some new collaborative book idea. Each of these amazing women agreed to go on this journey with us, and we are forever grateful. The moments of uncertainty have dissolved as each of their pieces you, dear reader, have just read lay before you. They agreed to expose some of the soft, uncomfortable truths of their experiences identifying and living as women. Our goal: to make the unknown known, to pull back the curtain

Z

and *unveil* things that weren't shared with us in our experience as women. We also worked to lean on the wisdom of multiple generations and hopefully to start a conversation that has long been needed among us women.

See, here's the thing: in a patriarchal society, those who identify as women often learn to define themselves in relation to the societal presentations of what defines a man. Every understanding of self, then, is measured by whether it is opposite enough while also being complementary and compatible enough to men. As these women share in all of their experience and stories, this effort to be just enough but not too much is a constant juggling act. This book aimed to make a statement of "enough is enough," and declare our own definitions of who and what we are as women.

We know we didn't cover it all, but we hope we pulled the curtain back enough to get you thinking and talking in your book clubs, your churches, your brunches, your walks, your wine downs, and all the other amazing things you do with your fellow female companions. I hope we leave you with a smile on your face and a greater appreciation for yourself, my dear, amazing, powerful, nurturing woman!

Meet the Authors

KRISTIN BOWEN, A DELAWARE NATIVE BORN and
raised in Wilmington, invites readers on a
transformative exploration of her life. From her
early days as a timid child with no voice to
becoming the fierce and confident woman she is
today, Kristin's journey reflects her commitment
to continuous growth and learning combined
with the power of unleashing trauma.

Kristin finds immense joy and comfort in her roles as a devoted
wife and mother to her four daughters, ranging in age from 7 to
18. Family holds a central place in her heart, and she cherishes the
precious moments spent together.

The writings included in this collaborative work serve as a
testament to Kristin's unwavering spirit.

Follow Kristin on Instagram @Kjacks99 or on
Facebook @Kristinbowen99.

TAYLOR EDWARDS IS A PROFESSIONAL MANAGER
who believes in the power of words. She lovingly
provides structure and organization around the
creative magic that is our Embodied Writing
Experiences. A writer, reader, and lifelong learner,
Taylor spends her time sponging up new
information, writing all she can, and spoiling her
two purr-fect cats. Connect with Taylor by following her blog,
housed at mytaylored.life.

MELISA GRAHAM IS A FREELANCE WRITER, ghostwriter, and editor with a background in marketing communications and self-assisted publishing. While much of her work is behind the scenes, her personal work has appeared in *Kakalak 2013*, *b2bTRIBE* magazine, and her small collection of poetry, *Used Cow for Sale*. She has two bio kids, three bonus kids, and a furbaby named Lola who is glued to her side. Connect with Melisa on LinkedIn and Instagram @1smelisa or on her website at melisagrahamcreative.com.

SHANA HARTMAN IS A FORMER UNIVERSITY English professor turned embodied writing coach. She helps heart-centered business owners and thought leaders share the core messages from their life and career experiences in powerful books by using an embodied writing approach that allows people to truly experience their transformative words. As a BodyMind Method© Coach, Shana supports folks in connecting with their inner truth and writing from that place (versus a set of external rules we think we should follow).

Learn more about Shana and the books her clients publish at shanahartman.com and follow her on Instagram @shanahartman_.

HAVING SPENT HER WHOLE LIFE IN school, Amanda Soesbee Kent currently teaches teenagers. Sometimes she teaches literature and writing, though usually her lessons are more about surviving life with sarcasm and wit. Amanda lives with her husband Bill on the family farm, where she collects rescue animals who serve no real purpose other than looking cute. Her major character flaw is believing that everything is within a 15 minute time frame, whereby she allows 10 minutes, hoping she can make it in 7. She has no plans to correct that flaw. However, she does plan to spend the rest of her career and life soaking up as many new books and producing as many new writings as she can, for her greatest love is words. You can follow her @Amanda.Soesbee on Facebook.

MACKENZIE URBANSKI MENON IS A RECENT graduate from UNC Chapel Hill with a major in Biology and minors in Chemistry and Linguistics because STEM major though she is, her English major parents rubbed off on her a little bit. Mackenzie currently resides in Philadelphia with her fiance and is a veterinary assistant for PASE  Animal Hospital in the Neurology Department. She is applying to veterinary school for the fall of 2024. Mackenzie loves cooking, being in the woods, a good book, quilting, and knitting. She can be found sharing all of the above with good friends and family. Connect with Mackenzie at amackenzie618@gmail.com.

RACHEL C. PATTERSON IS A BODYMIND Creative Coach, from the finger lakes region, who supports women in reclaiming their time and reigniting their creative spark. In her spare time, she can be found either playing with her puppy or creating unique gemstone fidgets and pendants. Learn more and connect with Rachel at bio.site/CohealingWellness.

TONYA REID IS A HAIRDRESSER BY trade who has always had a knack for entertaining and storytelling behind the chair. After raising her blended family of four boys with her husband, Billy Reid, and stepping away from her bustling

hair salon, she is enjoying having a damn minute to herself to get those thoughts on paper.

Being off-the-charts extroverted and passionate about supporting others' dreams, she is a powerful speaker and consultant. Connect with Tonya on Instagram @thetonyareid.

KAREN TAYLOR IS A PROUD MOTHER of a fine young man who served in the Marine Corps, and she is a dog lover to the point of ridiculousness. She loves reading books, spending time with her dogs, and basically being inappropriate. She is an English instructor at a community college in North Carolina and well known for being blunt, yet fiercely loyal to family, friends, students, and anyone who is a victim of a bully. You can connect with her on Instagram @taylor5869k.

CINDY URBANSKI IS A MOM OF three, for now. (She solidly counts her son-in-law to be as one of her children and hopes to add more to the brood someday when her son finds his person). She loves cooking wholesome food, reading good books, traveling and being in the woods or near the water with her husband and children. She is the Lead Writing Coach for Synergy Publishing and a Yoga instructor, both occupations that tap into her super power of helping people love on themselves. Cindy is fearlessly accepting, wildly authentic, persistently truthful, and relentlessly kind. Connect with her on Instagram @zen_by_u.

Acknowledgments & An Invitation

WE WANT TO THANK THE BRAVE women who answered our call to unveil their secrets. They made the book you are holding possible with their courageous and vulnerable words. It's no easy thing to share one's secrets, and each author did so in hopes of making the world a kinder, more transparent place to live. So, thank you to . . .

Kristin
Taylor
Melisa
Shana
Amanda
Mackenzie
Rachel
Tonya
Karen
Cindy

To Cindy, from Shana

Friend, we did it again! What a gift it is to walk with you through this journey of supporting others in sharing their powerful words! I'm so thankful for your leadership in this project as you kept up with deadlines, read (and reread and read again), gave helpful feedback, and steered all of us in the right direction during the creation of this book. Your vision for this book manifested in the most amazing ways, and I want to thank you from the bottom of my heart. What's next?!

To Taylor, from Cindy and Shana

Not only are you the glue that holds all the pieces and bits and bobs that we throw at you on the daily, you are a kickass writer, too! Thank you for helping us keep the guardrails on this project, the tech support, the reminders, and all the notes (because we forget all the smart things!). Your support is palpable, and we are so lucky to have it in all the amazing writing work we do.

To all our readers

We also believe that there are millions of others out there with secrets to share that could improve the world in which we live. Here's the invitation! It is our hope that you, dear reader, will share your secrets with us by following us on Instagram @shanahartman_ and sharing your own courageous and vulnerable story with us and tagging it #unveilingthesecrets.